Canadian Gardening's
WATER
in the GARDEN

By JANET DAVIS

with LIZ PRIMEAU *and* THE EDITORS *of* CANADIAN GARDENING MAGAZINE

A MADISON PRESS BOOK

Library and Archives Canada
Cataloguing in Publication Data

Davis, Janet (Janet M.)
Canadian gardening's Water in the garden /
Janet Davis.

Includes index.
ISBN 1-895892-42-2

1. Water in lanscape architecture-Canada.
2. Gardens-Canada-Design. I. Title.
II. Title: Water in the garden.

SB475.8.D38 2005   714
C2004-906286-7

Produced by
Madison Press Books
1000 Yonge Street, Suite 200
Toronto, Ontario, Canada
M4W 2K2

Printed in Singapore

Contents

Introduction

❦

Ponds and waterfalls used to be a privilege of the rich, but not any more. With today's submersible pumps and liners, anyone can make a water feature. My husband and I are living proof of this — we have two.

After we'd had a small, wood-framed pond sunk into our new deck, my husband confessed that what he'd really wanted was a natural-looking pond with a waterfall. "So I can hear the sound of water," he said.

He decided to make one himself. I came home to find him standing waist deep in an oval-shape hole in the ground, carefully fitting in PVC liner according to the instructions from a local pond-supply store. Soon he was adding a rock edging and a low waterfall. I offered to make a pebble beach, partly so  birds could hop to the water's edge for a drink, and partly because I was afraid the pond might end up looking like ... well, a hole in the ground outlined with rocks.

The pond is now well established, and my husband is rightfully proud of it. We dine beside it on hot nights, enjoying the cooling sound of water cascading over the rocks. On summer mornings, the fish swim up to greet us, mouths open in expectation of breakfast.

As my husband says, anyone can make a pond — as long as he has some expert advice! In *Water in the Garden, Canadian Gardening's* experts take you through the process step by step, from deciding on the perfect location and style to installing a liner and choosing the right pump. You'll also find practical information on filters, fish, plants and winter care, plus great ideas for small water features to enliven the tiniest garden, balcony or terrace.

Liz Primeau, Editor
Canadian Gardening Magazine

CHAPTER ONE

CASTING *a* SPELL WITH WATER

A pond
or other water feature,
no matter how small, makes any
city garden or expansive country
property a little more romantic,
a lot more animated and
infinitely more interesting.

WATER *in a* GARDEN

Water can be incorporated in a garden in countless ways. A formal reflecting pool, its tranquil surface a mirror of clouds and sky, might echo the classic lines of a stately stone home — while a natural pond edged with irises and rushes, where goldfish swim lazily beneath elegant water lilies, is the perfect complement to an informal garden.

Well-designed and skillfully integrated swimming pools, lap pools, hot tubs or plunge pools — although not water gardens in the classic sense — also have wonderful reflective qualities. The best marry function with form, proving every bit as ornamental as the prettiest lily pond.

Water adds to the seasonal appeal of a garden. In spring, a pond becomes a breeding ground for tadpoles and a watering hole for migrating birds. In summer, even the smallest water feature offers a cooling oasis from the heat of the day. And as the gardening year draws to a close, water captures the colorful splendor of

A birdbath is a simple way to bring the reflective quality of water into the garden.

autumn and the stark beauty of the frozen winter landscape.

If still water pleases, moving water pleases even more. Whether it's the splash of a waterfall tumbling down stepped rocks in a hillside garden, the gentle burbling of a wet millstone or the musical cascade of an elaborate fountain, the sound of water enhances the feeling of tranquility within the garden while dulling the din of traffic and noise outside.

For gardeners with limited space or budgets, or for those who like the *idea* of water but don't necessarily want to bother with digging and maintaining a pond, there are several less ambitious options. For example, a wall fountain can be purchased as a ready-to-install kit. All you need to do is attach it to a fence or wall, fill its basin with water and plug in the recirculating pump (which draws the water up from the basin through flexible tubing into a spout in the upper part of the fountain). Voilà — the splash of water without a waterfall.

A bamboo water spout splashes gently into a partially buried container water garden, offering the calming sound of water while creating a distinctly Oriental mood.

Or, you can create a small pebble pool by arranging decorative river rocks or smooth pebbles on a grate above an underground reservoir (a preformed pond shell is ideal) containing water and a recirculating pump. The pump, which is plugged into an outdoor receptacle, is fitted with flexible tubing that carries water up through the rocks, allowing it to bubble over them before returning to the reservoir. This simple pool can be conjured on even a small deck or patio.

And then there are birdbaths; ceramic pots large enough to hold a miniature water lily; Japanese-inspired bamboo spouts; stone basins; and half whiskey barrels big enough for a few goldfish. (For more on other water features, see p. 84.)

The possibilities for introducing

water into your garden are endless — as long as you remember to take the surroundings into account. Not every water feature is appropriate to every landscape. While birdbaths and basins will suit almost any garden, a waterfall or natural pond needs to be carefully planned and sensitively integrated.

By definition, of course, water gardening is inspired trickery. In the wild, a babbling brook doesn't start at the picket fence and come to a stop beside the garage. A natural waterfall tumbles down a rocky cliff because there's an immutable force of real, moving water at its back, not because there's a big recirculating pump at its base. And nature rarely plunks a wild pond in the middle of a tame lawn, surrounds it with petunias, fills it with a hodge-podge of aquatic plants and stocks it with a mini aquarium of fish and amphibians.

So how does the water gardener begin?

The answer is simple — by hiking along a mountain stream, walking through a natural marsh, sitting on a riverbank or on a dock beside a still northern lake. By going on garden tours, leafing through magazines, cutting out pictures and reading books like this one. And when all the research has been done, the wise gardener poses these two important questions: "What distinguishes my landscape? How can water, artificially introduced, enhance and improve it?"

Let's take a look at the way water has been incorporated in gardens throughout history. Then we'll help you discover the wonderful ways in which water can enhance and improve your own landscape.

Water Gardens
through the Ages

Decorative water features aren't new to gardens by any means. Villas in Pompeii, entombed by volcanic ash from Vesuvius in 79 A.D., were found to contain walled courtyard gardens, or peristyles, with pools and canals, some for catching rainwater from the roof. In ancient Persia, water was often featured in cruciform canals or in wall fountains with four symbolic water spouts — signifying the Persian belief in the four sacred rivers of life — that emptied into a basin below.

Baroque Italian Renaissance gardens, such as the Villa d'Este built in 1550, incorporated elaborate and often humorous water features, including cascading

stairways, spouting animal masks and even a hydraulically operated water organ that played music. In France, LeNotre's palatial gardens for Louis XIV at Versailles included the Parterre d'Eau, or water room, and numerous elaborate fountains.

England's Romantic landscape movement of the 18th century introduced more naturalistic water features, typified by William Kent's famous 1738 design for Rousham Park, which included Venus's Vale — a cascading water course that spilled through a forested hillside glade under stone arches into a pool below.

In Chinese landscapes, water and mountains predominated — water, as the *yin*, or soft female; rocky promontories, as the *yang*, or strong male presence. Ancient Chinese stroll gardens featured winding trails that moved from one carefully staged garden vignette — perhaps a waterfall or viewing platform overlooking a stream or tranquil pool — to another.

Water was also a vital component of Japanese landscape design. Even in gardens without a source of water, pebbles formed streams, and sand or gravel was carefully raked until its ridges resembled waves. Design guides for building waterfalls, dating from the 12th century, are still in use today, with styles such as heaven-falling (water from a high source), thread-falling (thin rivulets of water) and right-and-left falling (divided).

Not only was water itself integral to the Japanese landscape, the method of spanning it was also important. Stepping stones and arched moon bridges (which reflected in still water as perfect circles) were popular, as well as *yatsubashi*, zigzag bridges designed to deter evil spirits who were thought to be able to move only in straight lines.

Many modern Japanese gardens feature a *tsukabai*, or stone basin, used in temple gardens for handwashing before the tea ceremony.

CHAPTER TWO

WATER
in your
GARDEN

*A*t its best,
a pond or pool adds a pleasing
dimension to any garden. Depending
on its size, it may serve as a strong
focal point for the garden or
become the dominant element within the
landscape. It can also alter a site
optically, creating the illusion of more
space than actually exists.

CHOOSING A LOCATION
for a POOL OR POND

The primary reason for creating a water feature is aesthetic, so it makes sense to put a pool or pond where it enhances the landscape you have (or plan to have), and where you can see it easily from the house. You should also consider the particular pleasure you wish to derive from water in your garden.

If you'd like to enjoy the cooling effect of water close at hand, you might consider incorporating a water feature in a deck, terrace or patio. Or you might use the mysterious sound of water around a corner or at the end of a path as an irresistible destination in the garden, enticing visitors and drawing them closer.

If you want to create a natural pond that will attract a rich variety of wildlife, you'll need to situate it far enough away from the house to encourage visits. Most animals and birds are too wary of humans to approach a pond that's too close to the house.

But there's no design rule that says you must hide your water feature in the back yard. Why not put it right beside the entrance to your front door? A sophisticated

Incorporating a pond in a patio (left) or allowing it to flow like a lake under a deck (right) lets garden visitors enjoy the cooling effect of water close at hand.

shallow reflecting pool will distinguish your home from others and give it street appeal.

If you have children, you'll want to keep your pond in clear view. And if you want a pond deeper than two feet or so, and you live in a city that has by-laws governing swimming pool depths, you may have to fence your property and install padlocks on the gate. (See Safety Considerations with a Pond, p. 44.)

SUN *or* SHADE?

Since a pond should convey a sense of belonging in the garden, rather than being an isolated element, try to find a spot where it can be well integrated into the plantings around it.

Is the proposed site in sun or shade? Most flowering pond plants require considerable sun to perform well. Hardy and tropical water lilies (*Nymphaea* spp.) need six hours of sun daily, and the bewitchingly beautiful sacred lotus (*Nelumbo nucifera*) won't even consider unfurling its exotic chalices without soaking up several weeks of hot, sunny weather which has warmed water temperatures to a simmering 22°C (75°F).

In order to maximize sunshine for flowering aquatics, the pond should be located where tall trees and shrubs likely to cast shade during the hottest part of the day are to the north. It should also be protected from winds that can rough up the water surface and keep water lilies from flowering (they prefer still water to bloom).

But a shady property doesn't spell the end of water-gardening dreams. Yellow pond lily (*Nuphar advena*) is a native water lily relative that thrives in fairly shady ponds, producing modest tulip-like blooms and masses of foliage. Bog arum (*Calla pallustris*), marsh marigold (*Caltha palustris*), yellow flag iris (*I. pseudacorus*) and sweet flag (*Acorus calamus*) are marginal aquatic plants that also tolerate shade. Some lovely effects are possible using moisture- and shade-loving ferns and hostas, combined with Japanese primrose, Japanese iris, globeflower, astilbe and the bold architectural forms of rodgersia, ligularia and ornamental rhubarb. (For more on moisture-loving plants, see p. 65.) And shade has one major advantage — algae, which thrive in sunlight, are much less bothersome in a shady pond.

OTHER SITE CONSIDERATIONS

❧ Are there large deciduous trees nearby with surface roots that will make pond excavation a difficult or impossible task? Will their fallen leaves foul the water in autumn? Decomposing leaves can have a detrimental effect on fish health, particularly in winter when they release lethal methane gas as they break down.

❧ Certain types of trees and plants should be avoided near fish ponds. Pine needles and oak and maple leaves release tannic acid which, in heavy concentrations, can be toxic to fish; laburnum flowers and seeds are also poisonous.

❧ What about bedrock? Underground utility cables? Plumbing pipes? Digging a pond is difficult enough without unforeseen obstacles making things tougher.

❧ Topography is important, too. Do you have a sloping property, or a flat, featureless site? The bottom of a sharp slope is not always the best place for a small pond because it will receive run-off which can muddy the water or lift the liner. If you decide on a pond here, you may need to build it so that the back side of the pond is embedded in the slope, with the front raised above-ground. Run-off routes, gravel drainage sumps or plastic weeping tiles may also need to be installed so the pond isn't flooded by rain and melting snow. The advantage of a sloping property is that it's the perfect place for a waterfall.

❧ Is there a tap close enough to the site so you can easily fill and replenish the pond when necessary? Is there an electrical outlet close at hand to supply power for lighting or for a recirculating pump for a fountain or waterfall? If not, is it possible to run conduit containing the appropriate wiring underground from your house to the site?

A grounded electrical outlet in the garden permits the use of pump-dependent water ornaments, such as these spouting frogs.

FORMAL POOL *or* NATURAL-LOOKING POND?

Once you've decided where you'd like to situate a pond or pool, the next consideration is one of design. Of all the variables governing the creation of garden ponds and pools, the aesthetic ones are often the most difficult to achieve. Before you take shovel to hand, consider how water will fit into the existing landscape.

Is it appropriate to the garden? Is the style sympathetic to the architecture of the house? Is it an integral part of the property or a watery afterthought? In the final analysis, aesthetic considerations are as important as good workmanship.

Take a look at the architecture of your home and the style of your garden.

Do you have a formal Georgian or Tudor-style house with a wrought-iron fence, straight brick walkways and a manicured landscape of clipped hedges and tidy rose beds? An informal pond with sloping rocky banks, bulrushes and tadpoles would be jarringly out of place here. Instead, the setting suggests the symmetry and perfect geometry of a formal pool. It could be square, rectangular, oval or circular; in-ground or above-ground; lined with flexible pond liner or fashioned from granite, limestone, brick or cement. It might have a central fountain with water jets, feature a classic piece of statuary, or have stone-coped edges adorned with formal planters filled with flowers and trailing ivy.

A more contemporary house and a garden with informal plantings, on the other hand, lends itself to a naturalistic pond, which can be made to look as if it's always been there. If a wooden deck is already in place, additional decking can be extended over one or more edges of the pond to suggest a lakeside cottage dock. If the property borders on a meadow or woodland where a stream or bog garden can be contrived, so much the better.

On a brand-new property with few features and plantings, where the garden is being created from scratch, a naturalistic pond needs sensitive treatment with perennials, ornamental grasses, shrubs and trees that will grow quickly and be entirely appropriate to a waterside setting. Here, nature's own ponds can be used as a design guide. The advantage with a new garden, of course, is that the water feature can be the focus around which the rest of the garden is planned.

Without careful attention to the garden's theme, however, a pond or pool — even if it's finished with edging and plants that are in perfect harmony with its own style — can be inappropriate to the landscape. As tempting as it might be to introduce a Japanese-style pond, complete with river rock, koi, bamboo spout, water iris and stone lantern, in a traditional English border-style garden, the Japanese touch will always be the garden equivalent of a mixed metaphor.

WHAT ABOUT SIZE?

The ideal size for a naturalistic pond or formal pool is one that's in scale with the house and the property itself.

A country property with substantial acreage, particularly one with clay soil and naturally occurring springs, can

sustain a pond big enough for a canoe and swimming raft.

❧ Even a small property can generally accommodate a larger water feature than you might think, particularly if the water can be made to disappear like a lake under cedar decking or a stone terrace, or to meander around and through planted garden peninsulas.

❧ Size, of course, is relative. A small, watery oasis tucked like a jewel in a corner of a big city garden will be a delight, but a tiny pond installed in a vast putting-green lawn will look like a comic puddle.

❧ A narrow lot is ideal for a formal reflecting pool, rectangular in shape, contemplative in mood, overhung by lush plantings mirrored in the water's surface. If a rugged, natural look is more in keeping with the property, you might consider a narrow watercourse reminiscent of a windswept northern river, defined by rocky shores and laid on a gentle grade to keep the water moving.

❧ It's generally better for a pond to be too big than too small, since crowded conditions can soon tip the ecological balance (see A Short Course in Pond Ecology, p. 20.) The water in a small, shallow pool also heats up too quickly, jeopardizing fish. Once installed and stocked, a large pond isn't much more difficult to maintain than a smaller one.

❧ But if yours is a truly tiny property with a truly tiny garden, a pond can be as simple as a washtub sunk into the earth and planted with a single pygmy water lily, its edges disguised with trailing plants, its "shore" graced with a dimunitive shrub.

It's the quality, not the quantity, of water in a garden that's important.

A pond may be grandly formal (left), corresponding in style and size to an equally formal home and landscape — or it may nestle like a jewel in the tiniest shady nook.

AND SHAPE?

❧ A formal pool generally has a geometric shape — round, oval, rectangular, square, L-shape — and often mirrors the shape of nearby planting beds or walkways. It might be sunk into a formal lawn or paved terrace, or constructed partially or entirely above-ground.

❧ A natural pond has a curvilinear form, often interpreted as a crescent or kidney shape, and should mimic the random flowing shapes of nature's own ponds. Since a pond, by definition, is a natural depression filled with still water, the ideal location is in-ground with the water surface at the same level as the surrounding garden.

CHAPTER THREE

A SHORT COURSE *in* POND ECOLOGY

*$\mathcal{N}$ature has
perfected a system of checks and
balances for keeping pond life — fish,
animals, plants, nutrients, waste and algae —
in harmony. The successful creation and
maintenance of a pond depend on how
well the gardener understands and
imitates this ecosystem.*

THE ECOSYSTEM
of a POND

To enjoy pond gardening to its fullest and to maintain a healthy, balanced environment in and around the water, the wise gardener learns what each component of the ecosystem contributes to the mix, or bio-load; when and how to correct imbalances that might occur; and when to be patient and wait for nature to sort problems out. This is referred to as eco-balance.

Sunlight

All green plants need the sun's energy to fuel the process of photosynthesis. Chlorophyll and other light-capturing pigments in a leaf absorb and use sunlight to photolyze, or split, the water molecules the leaf receives from the plant roots into hydrogen atoms and molecular oxygen (O_2). At the same time, atmospheric carbon dioxide (CO_2) is absorbed through the pores, or stomata, in the leaf surfaces.

❀ During photosynthesis, the hydrogen and the carbon dioxide interact to make complex carbohydrates and simple sugars which are then used as food and building blocks by the plant. Oxygen essential to human survival is released into the atmosphere as a waste product of photosynthesis, which is why green leafy trees are often referred to as the earth's lungs.

❀ In a pond, photosynthesis in submerged oxygenating plants releases oxygen into the water during the day. At night, when the plants absorb oxygen to oxidize or metabolize plant sugars (called aerobic cellular respiration), carbon dioxide is released into the water. Submerged aquatic plants that don't have leaf stomata absorb gases and water over their entire surface. Some floating plants have stomata on the upper surface of their leaves.

❀ As well as providing the radiant energy for photosynthesis, the sun also stimulates flowering in all plants, including aquatics such as water lilies. But too much sun in a shallow pond can raise the water temperature to a level harmful to fish. The sun also promotes the growth of undesirable green algae, especially in spring. Therefore, it's usually recommended that 60 to 70 percent of a pond's surface be shaded by floating aquatic plants.

❀ Sunlight is also vital to the health of the oxygenating plants, which do their part in controlling algae by competing for the nutrients algae need to thrive.

Water

❀ Most municipal tap water contains chlorine, which kills bacteria that can be toxic to humans. But chlorine can also burn fish gills and harm aquatic plants. A volatile gas, chlorine dissipates into the atmosphere from standing water within 24 hours. However, to stabilize chlorine and make its effects long lasting, some water treatment plants also add ammonia to create chloramines. Ammonia at any level in a pond can be toxic to fish. Water containing chloramines should be treated with a chemical dechlorinator (e.g. *Aqua-Safe, Water Prep Plus*).

❀ When topping up a pond with tap water, spray the water into the pond with a hose nozzle to help aerate it. A submersible pump with a fountain jet or outlet that lifts water to the air also introduces oxygen, benefiting fish respiration and enabling microscopic nitrifying bacteria (see Fish, p. 25) to do their work. Try not to add more tap water than 5 to 10 percent of the pond's volume per week. Again, if a large fish population is present, use a dechlorinating product. If a large quantity of tap water needs to be added (for example, after repairing a leak), remove fish temporarily to an alternative holding tank containing reserved pond water.

❧ Rainwater, of course, offers a safe way of topping up a pond, and can be collected easily by placing a rain barrel under your roof's downpipe. Some cities now offer free programs to disconnect downpipes and hook up rain barrels.

❧ Water hardness is governed by the amount of calcium carbonate and magnesium present, and is measured on a scale from 1-30 dH (degree of hardness), with 1 degree equalling 17.1 ppm (parts per million) and 30 degrees equalling 535 ppm. Soft water is 4-8 dH, medium-hard is 8-17 dH and hard is 17-30 dH. Fish thrive at 3-12 dH (50-200 ppm) but a hardness up to 17 dH or slightly more is acceptable. Serious problems can arise with very soft water combined with very alkaline (high pH) conditions.

❧ Water pH is the degree of acidity or alkalinity and is measured on a scale of 1-14, with a reading of 7 being neutral. Acid conditions give a reading of lower than 7; alkaline is higher than 7. For fish, the ideal pH range is 6-8.5. Higher pH, or more alkaline conditions — which can be caused by leaching of calcium carbonate into a poorly sealed concrete pool or from concrete blocks — can cause fish stress, infections and death.

❧ Kits for testing pond water are available at water-garden suppliers.

Fish

Goldfish, koi and other ornamental fish bring a flash of color and a sense of play to a naturalistic pond. They're entertaining to watch and do their part in maintaining a pleasant garden environment by devouring mosquito larvae, which can be an annoying problem around still ponds. Fish also eat algae and may dine on the roots of some pond plants.

❧ But fish can upset the biological balance in a pond. Fish excreta is high in toxic ammonia and because fish won't survive in waste-polluted water, some means of reducing the ammonia level is needed. Ammonia is also food for algae. To curb ammonia, thus safeguarding fish and reducing algae, it's vital that a fish pond has sufficient levels of nitrifying bacteria to control algae growth.

❧ A certain level of nitrifying bacteria occurs in pond water naturally, but in a small, highly stocked fish pond where high levels of ammonia occur, it may be necessary to seed the pond with a beneficial bacteria additive, such as *Bacta-Pur Klear*. Large fish ponds require biological filtration.

❧ Because fish breathe by extracting oxygen from water drawn in through their gills, pond water must contain adequate oxygen. Oxygen is available from the air at the pond's surface but it's also supplied by submerged oxygenating plants (e.g., elodea, hornwort) and, to a lesser extent, by fountains or waterfalls which introduce oxygen by aerating the water.

❧ But even in a pond with a waterfall or fountain left operating during the night, fish are sometimes seen at the surface in the morning gasping for air. This happens because oxygen is depleted and high levels of carbon dioxide are produced — by the fish as they exhale and by the normal cellular respiration of plants during the night. In hot weather, particularly if there aren't enough floating plants (60 to 70 percent of the pond's surface) to keep the water shaded and cool, the water temperature will rise and oxygen will evaporate more quickly. At the same time, too many floating plants can prevent adequate absorption of oxygen through the water surface. To combat low oxygen levels, an air pump similar to an aquarium pump may be needed. Large fish ponds may require an air compressor.

Fish in a pond are both beautiful to look at and beneficial. By consuming mosquito larvae, they help maintain a pleasant garden environment.

Fish, especially koi, can muddy the water by rooting in the pots of marginal aquatic plants. Plants should be mulched with a layer of pea gravel or sand to prevent this.

In a pond with lots of plants and a small number of goldfish, fish food is not required — bugs, mosquito larvae, algae and some aquatic plants provide an ample diet. But if koi or a large number of smaller fish live in the pond, supplemental feedings are required. Because uneaten fish food can break down into ammonia and upset the water's balance, feed fish only what they can consume in 2 to 3 minutes.

To ensure fish stay healthy, it's important to keep their population at a safe level. Fish not only grow but spawn, especially if they're fed regularly; unfed goldfish usually consume their own eggs. Taking mature fish size into account, the standard rule in stocking a new pond is no more than 1 inch of fish per 2 square feet of surface area. Excess fish should be given away.

In a highly stocked fish pond, levels of ammonia, nitrite and nitrate should be measured regularly with a pond-testing kit (see p. 87).

Biofilters, Mechanical Filters *and* Ammonia Neutralizers

If you want a large number of fish, especially koi, you'll likely need a biological filtration system, or biofilter, that pumps pond water slowly through a special filtration medium — gravel, batting, cloth, sponge — which has been colonized by nitrifying bacteria. These bacteria normally occur in pond water but, to be truly effective in clearing waste, they should be concentrated in large numbers. In the filter media, they are safe from preying fish and well-supplied with oxygen from the pumped water.

Biofilters range in size from small models for 50- to 150-gallon ponds to large multi-arm models swathed in filter cloth for ponds of 1,500 to 1,800 gallons in size. External biological filters that move water past brushes and through various chambers are available for even larger koi ponds. Bubble bead filters handle up to 15,000 gallons.

To be effective, a biofilter must operate full-time, since shutting it down for more than a few hours can kill the nitrifying bacteria. The pump should allow the entire pond to recirculate slowly every 2 hours (for example, a 1,000-gallon pond should have a pump that recirculates 500 gallons per hour).

Because many biofilters are also mechanical filters (the reverse, however, is not true), they must be cleaned during the summer season, when water flow has slowed by about 25 percent. This should be done as quickly as

possible, using pond water to gently flush out sludge and debris. Do not scrub the filter, where the bacteria reside, and **never** use tap water.

❧ On its own, a biofilter is not intended to remove algae or suspended dirt particles, but it can be combined with an ultra-violet clarifier (UVC), which uses an ultra-violet lamp to clump together, or flocculate, algae and other single-cell particles. A strong ultra-violet light will also kill algae.

❧ Ammonia-neutralizing products such as zeolite can also be used, either in gravel form in an accessory container to your pump's mechanical pre-filter, in a nylon stocking bag suspended in the water, or in a block left on the pond bottom, where the nitrifying bacteria feed on it. Zeolite works on the principle of ion

Koi are notorious for browsing the roots of favorite plants, such as dwarf variegated Japanese sweet flag (above). Valuable plants can be protected with plastic-mesh fish barriers, available at water-garden suppliers.

exchange to attract ammonia, and must be recharged in a noniodized salt solution periodically.

❧ In a large pond with 60 to 70 percent of its surface covered with floating plants, oxygen is readily absorbed through the remaining surface water and is also produced by submerged oxygenating plants, so toxic levels of ammonia and carbon dioxide are unlikely. But problems will arise if nitrogen-rich lawn fertilizer leaches into the pond; water lilies are overfertilized; fish are overfed, or there are too many; or the pond is too shallow, too small or has too few floating plants to provide shade. Too many plants also create problems since they release an overabundance of carbon dioxide at night during photosynthesis, and block surface oxygen absorption.

Algae

Algae are the culprits responsible for turning pond water a pea-soup

A spring algae bloom has colored this Oriental pond pea-soup green. Green algae, while unattractive, generally disappear within a few weeks in an ecologically balanced pond.

green, especially in early spring as the sun warms the water. This phenomenon is known as an algae bloom or algae cycle, and is a normal part of a pond ecosystem. All ponds suffer from too much algae at some point.

🌿 Algae reproduce by spores which are everywhere on the planet. Not true plants at all, algae are plant-like micro-organisms or phytoplankton from the kingdom *Protista*. They occupy a lower rung on the evolutionary ladder than true plants, which belong to the kingdom *Plantae*. They are also at the bottom of the food chain, being the menu of choice for animal micro-organisms known as zooplankton, which, in turn, are eaten by fish.

🌿 There are more than 5,000 freshwater species of algae, but three are found in most ponds at one time or other.

Free-floating green algae cause the murky chartreuse water that appears

a few weeks after a pond is filled. It's mainly an aesthetic problem for the pond owner and does little harm to the pond, plants or fish. Left unattended, a green algae bloom will usually disappear within 4 to 6 weeks.

Brown (smooth) algae create the velvety coating on the bottom of the pond that makes you lose your footing as you step in to do maintenance. They also grow on pots, pumps and all pond surfaces. Eaten by fish, this algae is considered a sign of good pond health, rather than a problem.

Filamentous green algae (stringweed, blanketweed) are slow to develop but are often found attached to pond walls, wrapped around pots and water lily stems or floating on the surface. They clog pumps and are unattractive. Remove by twirling them around your finger or a stick and pulling them out. For a severe infestation, a new product called *Pond Balance* can be tried; used as recommended, it does not harm fish or plant life. In cool water, it takes 2 to 3 weeks for the desired effect, and repeat treatments may be required to keep filamentous algae from returning.

❧ Generally, algae have the same requirements as green plants — sunlight, air, water and nutrients. Although

algae may dominate the pond early in the season, when other aquatic plants are not established, they are soon deprived of food (nitrates) by submerged oxygenating plants such as elodea and hornwort. In summer, floating plants such as water lilies and water hyacinths have enough leaves to shade the water (depriving algae of sunlight) and to lower water temperature (algae like warm water).

❧ Natural inhibiting processes also take their toll. As algae multiply, so do their natural predators, the zooplankton. And algae's very success at colonization dooms them to death by overpopulation.

❧ Pond owners can prevent mid-season algae blooms by removing the faded flowers and yellowing foliage of pond plants, as well as any leaves blown in from nearby trees. In autumn, a net placed over the pond stops tree leaves from sinking to the bottom. It should be noted, however, that a perfectly clear pond will also provide a

Oxygenators

Oxygenating plants such as hornwort (*Ceratophyllum demersum*), sagittaria (*S. subulata*), Canadian pondweed (*Elodea canadensis*) and ribbon grass (*Vallisneria americana*) absorb nitrates that also stimulate growth of undesirable algae. They simultaneously release oxygen into the pond water, which can be seen as bubbles rising to the surface on a sunny day. The oxygen aids fish respiration and provides the aerobic conditions required for nitrifying bacteria to do their work.

❦ Depending on their growth habit, oxygenators are planted in pots or tossed into the water as cuttings. Because even rooted oxygenators absorb nutrients through their foliage, it is not necessary to plant them in soil — pea gravel is adequate. The recommended stocking level is one bunch of cuttings per 2 to 3 square feet of pond surface. To reduce the number of in-pond containers, some experts recommend planting rooted oxygenators in the same pots as water lilies.

❦ If a well-established algae bloom is present when you're adding oxygenators to your pond in spring, it may be necessary to place the potted ones nearer the sunny surface. (Oxygenating plants also provide an excellent habitat for spawning fish and a protective cover for fish fry.)

perfectly clear view of pots, pumps, cables and all the artifice that a pond owner may wish to hide.

❦ Pond water should **not** be changed to clear up an algae bloom. Tap water contains dissolved minerals — in other words, algae food — and starts the entire cycle all over again. Chemical algicides such as potassium permanganate and copper sulphate are not recommended because they can injure snails and slow the growth of aquatic plants.

❦ Operators of fish-free formal ponds at some botanic gardens — for example, Longwood Gardens in Pennsylvania — use an aquatic dye such as *Deep Water Shade* to combat algae. The dye prevents the specific light waves used by algae from fueling photosynthesis, ultimately starving the algae, but it does not affect the health of water lilies. The water appears blue-green in color, but it's clear rather than murky.

Snails *and* Tadpoles

Ramshorn snails (*Planorbis corneus*) and trapdoor snails (*Viviparis malleatus*) are beneficial scavengers in a pond, eating algae as well as decaying plant material and excess fish food. Snails should be added at the rate of one per square foot of pond surface. Because trapdoor snails bear their young live, unlike the ramshorn, which deposits its eggs in jellied masses under lily leaves, many gardeners prefer the trapdoors. Frog tadpoles also feed on algae and excess nutrients.

CHAPTER FOUR

CREATING
your
POND

*Before you put
shovel to earth, think about the type
of pond you'd like and where you'd
like to put it, then spend some time researching
the different styles and the cost of materials.
And keep in mind that the secret to
creating a successful pond is to make it look
like part of the landscape — a work of
nature, not of man.*

BEGIN *with a* PLAN

Building your own garden pond is an exciting process and the results will reward you with years of pleasure — but it's not something you want to do more than once! Sketching your ideas on paper and itemizing the features you want encourages you to develop a plan, even if some details have to be postponed until you have the budget to complete them. But first, study your property, determine how much sun and shade you have, and look out a window to decide where your pond should be sited for the best indoor viewing.

❧ If you want a waterfall, or think you may want one in the future, include that in the plan, too. (See Making a Waterfall, p. 50.)

❧ If you like the idea of sharing the pond with wildlife, plan to make a pebble beach on one side. Here, toads and frogs can crawl out of the water into the garden (they cannot climb vertical pond walls), birds can bathe and all manner of wildlife line up for a drink. Because a beach is difficult to add later, it should be part of the initial construction. (See Making a Pebble Beach, p. 59.)

❧ Plant lovers may want a bog garden adjoining the pond. Again, you don't have to install it right away, but it should be planned for as you design the pond. (See Making a Bog Garden, p. 63.)

❧ Pond drains and overflows are not generally necessary, but if you live in an area of high rainfall, you might have to plan for an overflow drain, pebble beach or bog garden.

❧ Don't skimp on size; try to relate the scale of the pond to your house and property. Make it a bit bigger than planned — it doesn't cost much more in labor or materials, and a bigger pond is easier to keep ecologically balanced.

❧ If you'd like a bridge, remember that it should actually lead to something on the other side of the pond — a bench, a gazebo or a path that leads into a garden. Since a bridge may require concrete footings at each end, you might need professional help with the construction. A Japanese-style timber or stepping-stone bridge can be supported by brick or cinder block piers under the water. Sometimes it's easier to *suggest* a bridge by building two ponds (one for fish, the other for plants) with an unexcavated section between them. Stepping stones or wooden decking can be added to give it the look of a bridge.

a round pool, use a string and compass point to circumscribe it accurately.

Outlining *and* Digging the Pond

Step I

❦ Whether you're making a natural pond or formal pool, outline the shape right on the ground using a clothesline, extension cord, hose or straight boards.

❦ For a natural pond, think in gentle, sweeping curves, avoiding sharp angles that look unnatural and prevent water from circulating freely. Simple shapes work best.

❦ For a formal pool in a square or rectangular shape, use a set square to make sure corner angles are 90°; for

Step 2

❦ Once you've settled on a shape you like, use spray paint to mark the outline on the ground.

❦ If you want planting shelves for marginal aquatic plants, it's a good idea to mark those too, as a simple reminder not to dig the entire pond at one depth. Many gardeners prefer to do without shelves because raccoons use the pots of plants as fishing perches, toppling them and muddying the water. On the other hand, most people have difficulty getting into a slippery pond to do annual maintenance without a shelf to step on.

❦ A good depth for growing water lilies and stocking goldfish is 18 to 24 inches (45 to 60 cm). To overwinter fish and lilies, a deeper water level is required, 3 to 6 feet (1 to 2 m), depending on the frost zone in your area. If you plan to stock koi, which need ample space as well as substantial vertical swimming depth, the pond should have an area 3 to 4 feet (1 to 1.3 m) deep, more if they are to overwinter in the pond (see Koi, p. 82). Remember that a pond deeper than 2 feet (60 cm) may be subject to swimming pool safety bylaws (see Safety Considerations, p. 44).

❦ Before you dig, and especially if you hire a backhoe to dig a large pond, make sure you know where utility cables and pipes are. Damage incurred during the excavation is your liability.

A shallow depression around the pond rim allows edging stones to sit right at water level, rather than perched above.

Step 3

❧ Begin to dig in the center of the pond and move to the edges. Cut away turf first and put it on the compost, or turn it upside down as a base for a waterfall if you're building one. Put topsoil on a tarp or plastic sheet to use in the planting area around the pond.

❧ The subsoil below is heavy and often contains clay; while satisfactory as a waterfall foundation, it should be amended with lots of organic material (peat moss, compost, leaf mold) before it's used in the garden. However, with the addition 1:1 of rich garden loam (but not peat moss or compost, which float away), it's fine as a base for potting water lilies and aquatics, which need rich, heavy soil.

❧ Water always finds its own level, so if the rim of your excavation isn't level, the water will appear to be deeper in some areas than others, leaving the liner exposed. To check, lay a long board topped with a carpenter's spirit level across the pond in several spots. To equalize, it's better to level areas that are too high rather than to add soil to lower levels.

❧ The pond bottom should slope gently at an angle of about 10° to the deepest area, where the pump and/or

biofilter will be located.

❧ Apart from a pebble beach, which requires a gently sloping bank on a very wide shallow shelf, pond walls should be built on an almost vertical angle to prevent the liner from showing once the edging is in place. Slope the walls about 1 inch for every 3 inches of drop (1 cm per 3 cm drop), or about 20° (as in drawing, above). The liner will be visible if the wall slopes too much.

Step 4

❧ As you dig, measure the depth periodically with a yardstick or board marked at the desired level. Planting shelves for marginal aquatics should be about 12 inches (30 cm) wide and 8 to 12 inches (20 to 30 cm) from the surface, and they can circle the entire pond or just a portion. Some gardeners dig planting basins at various depths in the pond bottom and, once the liner is in place, fill them with heavy soil for direct planting.

❧ To make the edging look natural, dig a shallow shelf for the flagstones, boulders or whatever you plan to use, so the edging will sit *at* ground level, rather than *above* it. (Continue to check with a spirit level that the rim is level.)

Lining *and* Edging *the* Pond

Step 1

❧ Once the pond is dug, measure the surface area and the depth, adding irregular areas such as a waterfall, gravel beach, bog garden or planting basins on the pond bottom, to determine the size of liner and geotextile underlay you'll need. Extra underlay will be required as protective matting for waterfall and edging rocks.

❧ Don't skimp. While our formula for calculating the amount of liner you'll need (see box, below) provides more than enough for trimming back at the edge, it's always better to err on the generous side. Scrap pieces of underlay can be used under edging stones or as underwater cushioning for plant pots.

Step 2

❧ Even if you use an underlay, some roots and rocks are eventually going to move upward through the soil, so it's a good idea to add a protective layer of sand beneath the liner.

❧ Smooth a 2-inch (5 cm) layer of damp sand over the entire excavation. If you're not using an underlay, cover the sand with old carpet pieces or several thicknesses of newspaper. Unlike underlay, these eventually break down, but they're better than nothing.

❧ If you're using a commercial underlay, unfold it in the excavation, smooth out the wrinkles and pleat it carefully at the top. Don't cut off the excess yet.

Step 3

❧ Spread the liner out on your patio or lawn. Let it warm in the sun so it becomes pliable, but don't leave it on the grass in the sun for more than an hour or so, or the grass may burn under its heat. When the liner is flexible, maneuvre it into the excavation, allowing an even overlap on all sides. (This is usually a two-person job, and best done in rubber boots or soft-soled running shoes.)

❧ For larger ponds, where spreading out the liner first is not practical, lay the liner directly in the excavation and leave it for an hour or so. It will still warm sufficiently and become flexible enough to maneuvre.

Step 4

❧ Drape the liner in the hole. Smooth it down across the pond floor (and into any planting basins), removing as many air pockets as you can. Spread it upward over the walls and shelves, pleating it as you go. Don't worry if the pleats aren't smooth and flat. When the pond is filled, the pressure of the water will press the liner against the walls.

Step 5

❧ Once you've smoothed out the liner on the pond floor, place a few

---

HOW MUCH LINER *will* I NEED?

To calculate the amount of liner and underlay required, take the length at the longest point + twice the depth + 2 feet. Calculate the width the same way. For example, if your pond is 9 x 12 feet and 18 inches deep, you'll need a liner about 17 feet x 14 feet.

CALCULATIONS
Length: 12 + 2(1.5) + 2 = 17 feet
Width: 9 + 2(1.5) + 2 = 14 feet

stones on the liner around the rim to hold it down as you start filling the pond with water. If your home has a water meter, this is a good time to determine your pond's volume. Check the reading before and after filling the pond. Make sure no water appliance — a shower or washing machine, for example — is being used at the same time. (For a mathematical calculation of pond volume, see next page.)

With a flexible liner, you can create any design and the pond can be as deep as you like. Once the hole is dug, use commercial underlay or newspaper to protect liner. Fit liner into place and partly fill with water to tighten.

❦ Continue smoothing the liner to the top, moving the stone weights as you go. Work from the rim if you can, or by standing in the pond (wearing rubber boots, of course). It's important to try to press the pleats as firmly as you can, but every lined pond has a few bulky folds. Don't worry — they won't show once the pond has been filled and the edging is in place.
❦ Although there are no hard and fast rules for lining a pond,

the reason for putting water in the bottom before the liner has been completely fitted at the top is to use the water's weight to push the liner into the excavation. Turn off the water if you think you need more time to smooth the folds.

Step 6

❦ Once the pond is almost full, remove the stone weights and start putting the edging or coping stones in place (see Edging a Pond, p. 41).
❦ Arranging edging stones to cover the liner is a matter of trial and error. Fitting cut flagstones together is a little like doing a jigsaw puzzle. With smooth river rocks or larger boulders, it's important to create as natural an effect as possible, perhaps by carrying the rock motif into the garden or the waterfall. Edging rocks should overhang the rim in a cantilevered effect so the liner doesn't show. Don't cut off excess liner at the top just yet.

Step 7

❦ When you're happy with the edging, lift up the rocks and trim back the liner and underlay to fit neatly under them. Replace the edging. If desired, wet mortar may be used between rocks to glue them in place.
❦ Wait 24 hours after filling the pond before putting in plants. Use a dechlorinating product before adding fish.

LINERS *and* UNDERLAYS

Theoretically, you can use any flexible waterproof sheeting or membrane to line your pond, but not all liners are created equal.
❦ **Clear polyethylene plastic sheeting** is inexpensive and extremely flexible but punctures easily and decomposes within a few years.
❦ **PVC (polyvinyl chloride) flexible liners** are widely used. They're non-toxic, resilient, reasonably priced and most are UV-stabilized to withstand the sun's ultraviolet rays. Most also come with a 10-year warranty, and simple tears can be patched with custom adhesive. Thickness varies from 20 to 40 mil; there are 1- and 2-ply types as well. But PVC has some disadvantages. It can't be stretched and it's sometimes hard to fit it in an excavation, particularly the 2-ply 40-mil type. And in very cold climates, PVC can become brittle over time and crack.
❦ **EPDM (ethylene propylene diene monomer)** is a synthetic rubber liner that's flexible, UV-stabilized, stretchable, withstands cracking to -70°C and usually carries a 20-year warranty. EPDM liners were developed as a low-talc version of a roofing material and are not toxic to fish or plants. Some water-garden suppliers now stock EPDM exclusively, believing it to be superior (though moderately higher priced) than PVC. It comes in stock sizes up to 50 x 200 feet (15 x 60 m), but larger sizes can be joined by heat-fusing.
❦ The best protection for a pond liner is a synthetic fabric underlay, called a geothermal textile or geotextile.

Preformed Pond Shells

Moulded ponds are trickier to install, but they're easier to repair if pierced. The form should sit on a level base, with the rim slightly above grade. Backfill firmly.

Preformed fiberglass and polyethylene pools are available in a variety of styles and sizes — from freeform and kidney shapes (some with shelves for aquatic plants) to square, rectangular, octagonal, circular or L-shape for more formal settings.

Prices for fiberglass are higher than polyethylene. Although both are UV-stabilized, fiberglass is a stronger product with a longer life expectancy (50 years); it can also be used above ground. Depths vary from 12 to 18 inches (30 to 45 cm).

Deeper models are best for water lilies and also for fish, which can suffer from overheating in shallow pond shells.

HOW DO I CALCULATE *the* VOLUME *and* SURFACE AREA OF MY POND?

Knowing the approximate volume of your pond helps you decide on the most efficient pump and filter. Knowing the correct surface area is important in stocking fish and oxygenating plants.

For a Rectangular or Square Pond
❧ To calculate the volume, first multiply length at the longest point x width at the widest point to get the surface area. Then multiply the surface area x depth to get the cubic feet. Then multiply cubic feet x 6.25 for Imperial gallons, x 7.5 for U.S. gallons.

For example, for a pond 8 feet wide x 10 feet long x 2 feet deep:
Multiply 8 feet x 10 feet
= 80 square feet surface area
80 square feet x 2 feet depth
= 160 cubic feet
160 cubic feet x 6.25
= 1,000 Imperial gallons

For a Circular Pond
❧ To calculate the volume, multiply the pond diameter by itself, divide the answer by 2, and multiply that by 3.14 (22/7 or *pi*).

For example, for a pond 8 feet in diameter and 2 feet deep:
Multiply 8 feet x 8 feet
 = 64 feet surface area
64 divided by 2
 = 32
32 x 3.14
 = 100.5 cubic feet
100.5 cubic feet x 6.25
 = 628.12 Imperial gallons

INSTALLATION

❧ Lay the shell on the site. Use chalk or spray paint to outline the top and bottom shapes.

❧ Dig the hole a few inches bigger than the pond shape, sloping in the sides and contouring shelves as required. Both top and bottom must be level, so work with a long board and carpenter's level, as with a flexible liner.

❧ Dig down 2 inches (5 cm) deeper than the pond's depth. (Preformed shells should sit slightly above the soil level to prevent surface run-off from muddying the water.) Compact the soil at the base well, removing all roots and rocks. Add a 3-inch (5 cm) layer of sand under the shell, wetting it to keep it in place.

❧ Lay the form in and move it back and forth, making sure it makes contact everywhere. Make sure the bottom is level and backfill with more sand, if necessary.

❧ Fill with water while simultaneously backfilling the sides and tamping down. Finish with desired edging, taking care not to put pressure on the rim.

EDGING *a* POND

Where soil is sandy or there is likely to be heavy foot traffic on the pond rim, a base course of one or more layers of flagstones or pavers provides a solid foundation under the edging stones.

The edging or coping you use around your pond's perimeter should hide the liner. Natural rock or boulders also help create the illusion that the pond is a natural form.

❧ The type of edging you choose should correspond to other hard landscaping materials in the garden. If the pond adjoins a patio made of flagstone, it makes sense to use a flagstone edging. Boulders convey a more rugged feeling and can be combined with smooth river rocks in graduated sizes to suggest an alluvial mountain stream. Large, flat, granite rocks make a good edging for a big pond, particularly one with a granite slab waterfall. For a formal pool, flat pieces of limestone, sandstone or Pennsylvania bluestone, along with brick or granite setts, make an elegant coping and convey formality. Concrete patio slabs are very inexpensive and give a crisp edge to a formal pond.

❧ If your soil is sandy, or if there is likely to be heavy foot traffic on the pond's edge, you may wish to add a layer of gravel or a second course of flagstone or concrete pavers underneath as a foundation for the edging stones. If you do this, tuck the pond liner *under* and *behind* the foundation course, then fold it *over* at the top before covering it with the coping stone, as in the drawing below. (Whenever you place stone on top of the liner, remember to use a piece of underlay to protect the liner from punctures.) Although this method is more expensive, the extra course of rock gives a naturalistic look to the inner edge of the pond and provides a firm foundation.

❧ Another means of reinforcing the edging stones is to use a thick layer of gravel underneath them, or to stiffen the soil below by adding dry ready-mix cement in a 1:8 cement-to-soil ratio. The pond walls can also be reinforced inside the liner by stacking cinder blocks that have been filled with gravel.

❧ Plants used as edging often make as big an impact as stones. Rugged creeping shrubs such as prostrate cotoneaster, bearberry (*Arctostaphylus*) and stephanandra; small conifers and dwarf broadleaf evergreens such as boxwood and rhododendron; and scrambling flowering plants like lady's-mantle, forget-me-not and mimulus are very effective at the edge of a pond.

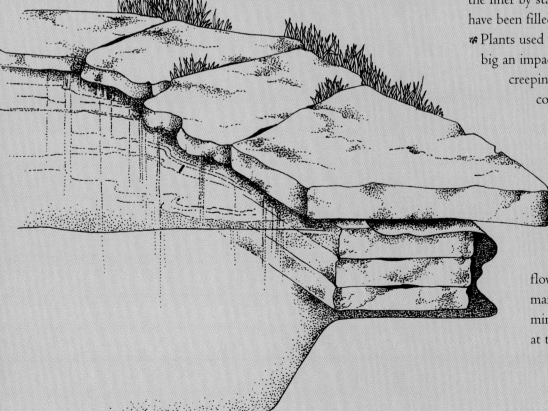

A FORMAL CONCRETE POOL

Concrete as a building material for ponds and pools has been largely eclipsed by flexible and preformed pond liners, which are much less work. Poorly constructed concrete ponds often crack in winter because the walls are either too thin or are not reinforced well enough to withstand the pressure of ice as pond water freezes. (Cracking can be prevented to a large extent by partially emptying the pond in winter.)

Still, some gardeners prefer concrete, particularly for a raised, geometrically shaped pool. Concrete gives an air of permanence; when faced with stone, tile or brick, it is very appropriate to a formal garden. However, concrete construction is exacting and not always for the do-it-yourself pond builder. Swimming-pool contractors will usually quote on an ornamental garden pool; a generous budget might even allow for Gunite, a sprayed concrete product that allows both walls and floor to be built without a seam.

A landscape architect and a swimming-pool contractor collaborated to create this striking concrete pool in a formal garden in Toronto.

SAFETY CONSIDERATIONS WITH *a* POND

GENERAL SAFETY

❧ Be cautious with water features, especially deep ones, that flow under decking, bridges, or immediately adjacent to walkways, decks or terraces. They are dramatic but dangerous, and the pond owner is responsible and liable. Construct a railing or use a planter box to delineate the edge. Keep a life ring nearby.

❧ Ensure that ponds and pools at ground level are well-lighted to prevent accidents at night.

ELECTRICITY

❧ Check local electrical codes when installing wiring outdoors. There may be a required minimum distance from the water for an outlet for lighting or for a recirculating pump.

❧ Make sure all underground wiring is contained within a PVC conduit pipe. Mark all wiring routes on a diagram to be kept in your files.

❧ Make sure all wiring, outlets, timers, pumps and filters are CSA approved. Ensure that electrical receptacles have GFI (ground-fault interrupter) devices, and that all electric components have 3-prong grounded plugs.

❧ Water and electricity can be a dangerous — even lethal — combination. Unless you are experienced, hire a professional to do the wiring. A 12-volt system is less dangerous to install and operate.

❧ Don't enter the pond to do any maintenance until you have turned off the pump and/or any other electric components underwater.

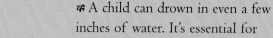

CHILDREN

❧ A child can drown in even a few inches of water. It's essential for every water gardener to make sure that his pond or pool does not have the potential for tragedy.

❧ A deep pond is not recommended if there are small children in the family or immediate neighborhood, unless the pond area is fenced and has a self-locking gate.

❧ If you move into a house with a pond and have small children, consider turning the pond into a sand box. You can resurrect the pond, if desired, when the children are older.

❧ A special PVC grid can be cut to fit just below the pond surface, anchored onto foundation rocks. This will provide an element of safety and, if the grid is large enough, will allow fish to swim at ease while preventing predators from reaching them.

❧ Some cities have safety by-laws that govern all swimming pools and ponds. In one city, a pond more than 2.2 feet (66 cm) deep is deemed a privately owned swimming pool, for the purposes of the by-law. In another, the depth is 2 feet (60 cm). Check with your local building codes office to see if fencing and a gate are required.

Small children should never be left unattended near a garden pond.

Landscaping *the* Pond

*Positioning plants, such as the dwarf hemlocks (above)
or the hosta (below), right at the water's edge creates a beautiful reflection while
integrating the pond into the surrounding garden.*

To make an attractive transition from the pond to the surrounding landscape, the gardener can choose from a huge palette of flowering and foliage perennials, ornamental grasses, conifers, flowering shrubs and trees. Restraint is key; try to avoid planting one of everything. The reflective quality of still water has the strongest impact when brilliantly colored plants are massed in drifts, or when bold foliage forms and architectural shapes are allowed to dominate rather than compete with others.

❧ To suggest a natural setting for your pond, try to obscure the artificial boundaries and features in your garden. Disguise fences and garage walls with evergreen hedges (cedar, laurel, yew, hemlock) and lush vines (trumpet vine, euonymus, Virginia creeper).

❧ Avoid the fish-pond-in-the-lawn syndrome by setting the pond in its own landscape to separate it from the manicured lawn. And try not to resort to bedding plants like petunias, impatiens or snapdragons near the pond — save those for the flower beds.

❧ If your pond has an Oriental theme, carry it through to the landscape. Choose elegant, understated plantings that convey a feeling of tranquility. Weeping trees have a special affinity to Oriental gardens, and look charming with branches draped over still water. Consider weeping cultivars of Japanese cherry, katsura, ginkgo, white pine, crab apple and Japanese maple.

❧ Other plants for an Oriental-theme water garden include sculptural ornamental grasses such as maiden grass, Japanese blood grass and, where hardy, the various bamboos. Appropriate shrubs include rhododendrons, azaleas, sumac, boxwood, cotoneaster and mugho pine. Hostas and ferns combine with lovely water irises — yellow flag, Japanese and Siberian.

❧ There are numerous trees, shrubs and perennials suitable for a natural pond. However, the objective for many pond gardeners is to create a waterside setting that nature herself might have designed. Obviously, that means native plants, so the gardener should consult a good local reference, paying close attention to riparian species — those adapted to life beside a watercourse.

❧ Good shrub and tree cover, plants with berries, and the sound of running water attract a variety of birds to eat and bathe at a sunny pond. A big pond might even bring yellowthroats, kingfishers, song sparrows and red-wing blackbirds.

A burgundy-leafed Japanese maple combines with iris, cedars and mossy rock to enhance the Oriental theme of this water garden.

❧ Native trees for a sunny pond garden include river birch, trembling aspen, red maple, blue beech or ironwood, tamarack, chokecherry, pin oak, Canada plum and various native thorn trees. A selection of native shrubs might include elderberry, buttonbush and winterberry. Shrubs with brilliant autumn color to reflect in the water include sumac, chokeberry, summersweet (*Clethra* spp.) and many excellent serviceberries (*Amelanchier* spp.).

❧ Numerous sun-loving ornamental grasses, sedges and rushes are suitable in your pond plantings, but there is one to avoid. Common reed (*Phragmites australis*) is a tall, vigorous, invasive grass that has naturalized worldwide but offers neither food nor habitat to wildlife, and excludes native plants.

❧ Weeping willow is a romantic waterside tree for lakes and parks, but it's too weak-wooded and root-invasive for most gardens. And as pretty as they are, purple loosestrife species *Lythrum salicaria* and *L. virgatum* and all their garden cultivars should be avoided to curb their rampant invasion of natural wetlands.

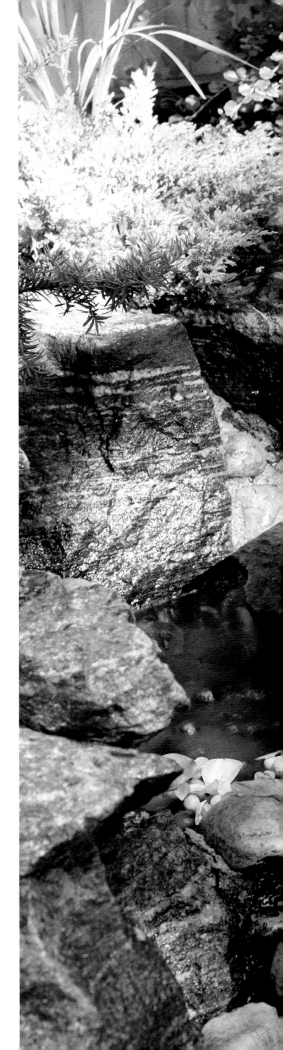

CHAPTER FIVE

ADDING FEATURES

*Whether you
choose a waterfall splashing over carefully
placed rocks, a pebble beach to
attract birds and frogs, or a bog garden
filled with moisture-loving plants,
here's how to add to the magic of
water in your garden.*

MAKING *a* WATERFALL

Waterfalls are often used in large gardens to exploit natural level changes or as part of a hillside rock garden. But any garden can incorporate a small waterfall as a lively addition to a naturalistic pond, and even the smallest garden is enhanced by the sound of water trickling over a cairn of rocks. Ultra-modern architectural styles or commercial landscapes may suggest a less nature-based approach — a water wall, for example, where water flows down the face of a granite or marble slab in perfectly symmetrical fashion, in tune with the other built features.

Apart from their aesthetic role, waterfalls aerate and improve the ecological quality of pond water. In small waterfalls, a lower pond contains the submersible pump, which forces the water via flexible reinforced tubing back to the top. A longer waterfall requiring a large volume of water may need a powerful external pump. A waterfall descending through more than one pool might require a submersible pump for each pool.

You can build a waterfall from scratch to suit the contours of your garden (right), or you can save time and labor by incorporating a prefabricated stone waterfall unit (below), available in a variety of styles from water-garden suppliers.

Before *you* Start

Waterfalls often fail for two reasons. First, they can sometimes spring leaks. This was a more common problem in the days before flexible pond liners and preformed waterfall units made from fiberglass or reconstituted stone, when concrete was the only viable means of construction and winter-cracking was a common occurence. However, even a lined waterfall can leak if the liner is pierced by sharp rocks, or if the flow of water is not properly channelled forward.

Second, waterfall builders often get to the very end of the project, only to find that the water level in the catchment pond drops too drastically because the watercourse is too high or too long, or the pump is too small or too big. Obviously, a large waterfall requiring powerful external pumps is not a task for the average home gardener; help from a landscape professional might be advisable.

Site *and* Design Considerations

❧ A pond with a waterfall should be big enough to allow the water to enter without causing turbulence near water lilies, which flower only in quiet water. Some gardeners install a small, separate catchment pond for the waterfall, then drop to a larger pond containing lilies and aquatic plants.

❧ The waterfall should enter the shallowest part of the pond, opposite the end containing the recirculating pump. Remember, too, that a waterfall should appear to be falling naturally from higher ground. Leave enough space behind it to disguise the source and all the mechanics with well-placed rocks, trees or shrubs.

❧ If you have a natural slope or hillside rock garden behind the pond, work with the grade to create a natural-looking waterfall — installing the liner and disguising it with rocks to form a cascade, possibly from small pool to small pool, until it finally empties into the base pond.

❧ If you don't have a slope, you can still have a waterfall by designing either an artificial hill made from excavated pond soil (see instructions, next page) or, even simpler, by building a low cairn of rocks. Bring a length of tubing up and out of the pond, thread it through the edging rocks and lay it atop the rocks piled on the pond edge. Cap the end of the tubing, poke a few holes into the lower front part of it, back it with a length of pond liner so the water doesn't flow backward, then turn on the pump to see how it flows. After adjusting the flow by adding more holes, camouflage the tubing with another layer of rocks.

A feathery Japanese maple disguises the source of this tiny waterfall.

Constructing *a* Lined Waterfall *from* Pond Subsoil

Step 1

❧ Place a length of flexible tubing in the pond and attach one end to the pump. The pump should be raised from the pond bottom on a brick to prevent silt and sediment from entering. (To determine the right pump for the waterfall, see box below.) Don't cut the tubing too short; leave enough to play with as you design your cascade. Black anti-kink reinforced tubing is preferable to clear PVC tubing (which permits algae growth that clogs the tubing). Reinforced tubing comes in several diameters, but 3/4-inch to 1-1/2-inch is usually sufficient.

Step 2

❧ Once you've chosen a spot beside the pond for your waterfall, begin mounding the subsoil removed from the excavation. Make sure the soil is well compacted; if it's light or sandy, you may need to make a thick (12-inch) concrete footing to prevent shifting and you may need to reinforce the inside of the mound with cinder block. The mound should be in scale with the size of the pond, and up to 3 feet (1 m) high for a single pump.

❧ Thread the tubing just under the soil and have it come out at the top.

Step 3

❧ Using a shovel, cut out a depression for the top, or header pool, and carve out a few steps or levels down to the pond. The steps should funnel slightly away from the walls and slope gently backward, so some water stays in each section if the water is turned off. Each level should have a vertical drop of between 6 and 12 inches (15 to 30 cm).

Step 4

❧ Once the levels are dug, install the underlay (if you're using it), then line each level with pond liner. Use a separate piece of liner for each level, moving from bottom to top and making sure each piece generously overlaps the next so water can't escape backward. To further ensure against leakage, liquid pond liner or waterproof tape can be used on liner joints. Don't let the geotextile underlay touch the pond water; capillary action can suck water out.

❧ The sides of the liner should be high enough that water won't seep sideways into the soil or splash out.

SELECTING *a* PUMP *for a* WATERFALL

Your water-garden supplier can help you choose the best pump for the height and width of your waterfall, along with the rate of flow you prefer.

❧ As a rule, a 1-inch-wide stream of water flowing over the edge of a waterfall 1/2 inch deep equals 100 gallons per hour. To calculate the number of gallons per hour (GPH) for your waterfall, multipy this figure (100 gallons) by the width of your waterfall face.

For example, a 12-inch-wide face = 12 x 100 gallons per hour = 1200 GPH. Therefore, you will need a pump that moves 1200 gallons per hour (GPH).

❧ If your waterfall is 3 feet high, you will need a pump that lifts 1200 GPH to a height of 3 feet. For a less forceful rate of flow, a slightly smaller pump can be used.

For a waterfall, use soil removed from the pond to build up a small rise — for a natural look, keep the water course low. Starting at the base, overlap pieces of liner over the soil and disguise with stones and plants. Sand or pebbles will hide liner underwater.

holes and slits so the water flows in a wider face. Or you can fit the end of the tubing into a PVC tube — capped and drilled at the front with several holes — to distribute the flow.

❧ Use rocks to camouflage the tubing at the top, and half-bury some in the earth mound for planting later.

Step 6

❧ When you're satisfied with the water flow, remove the rocks and reset them in very thick mortar or in a bed of spray-on polyurethane foam — *Dap* and *Mono* are available at most hardware stores. Use the mortar or foam to fill in the spaces between the rocks and prevent the water from running behind, instead of over, rocks.

❧ Poly foam expands to 40 times its volume, is frost-proof (unlike cement or mortar) and adheres very well to the pond liner. But wear gloves; poly foam can burn your hands. Add pebbles or sand while the foam is still wet to give it a more natural look, or paint it when dry with a non-toxic waterproof latex paint.

Step 5

❧ Place flattish spillway stones at the edge of each level, tilting each a little forward and chiselling grooves if necessary to make sure water flows well. Fill in each level with more of the same kind of stones, or use rockery stones, cobbles or boulders to achieve a natural look.

❧ Protect the liner from punctures by using pieces of underlay or special protective rubber pads under waterfall rocks.

❧ Turn on the pump and experiment with the flow, moving the rocks about until you're satisfied.

❧ Rather than having a single, concentrated flow from the end of the tubing, you may wish to lay the tubing horizontally across the top of the waterfall, cap the end, then puncture it with a series of smaller

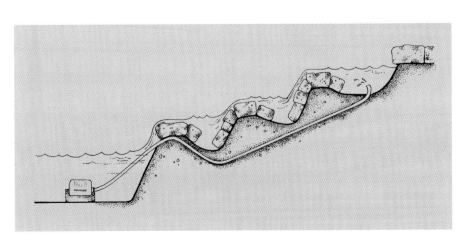

Planting *the* Waterfall

Unless a man-made waterfall cascades down a natural slope, it needs clever planting to disguise the fact that it's been fashioned from a disconnected mound of earth or rocks, without a natural beginning or end to its flow.

❧ Disguise the source with conifers such as spruce, hemlock, false cypress or cedar. Even a feathery Japanese maple can effectively hide the mechanics of construction.

❧ On a small waterfall slope, squat shrubs are better than big ones: nest spruce, fragrant sumac, dwarf junipers, spireas and boxwood. Grasses might include smaller species such as Japanese sedge (*Carex morrowii*), blue fescue or Skinner's brome (*Bromus inermis* 'Skinner's Golden').

❧ In the soil pockets around the waterfall, plant bulblet ferns (*Cystopteris bulbifera*), which quickly colonize rocky places. Tuck damp moss into nooks and crannies, and use easy-care ground covers such as bugleweed, Irish moss, creeping Jenny, dwarf campanulas, knotweed, barrenwort, thyme, low sedums and hostas.

Bergenia, lady's-mantle, primroses and Siberian iris soften the rugged look of a granite-slab waterfall (below).

MAKING *a* PEBBLE BEACH

In the stream-like shallow pond at left, pebbles and smooth rocks were placed on top of the pond liner to form the gently sloped shores and floor. Alternatively, a simple pebble beach can be fashioned on a wider underwater shelf in the pond, as illustrated below.

Rather than having straight walls around the entire pond, consider turning one side into a gently sloped pebble or gravel beach.

A beach encourages wildlife to visit the pond. It also integrates the pond into the garden, provides an overflow area for pond water during heavy rains and allows toads and frogs to leave the water once they've evolved from the tadpole stage.

As you dig the pond, make a shelf — 2 feet (60 cm) wide and as long as you want the beach to be — approximately 6 inches (15 cm) below the pond rim. At the front edge, lay a curb of stones or bricks on end, covering it with extra underlay to avoid puncturing the liner.

When it's time to put the underlay and liner in place, spread them over the curb and the shelf, leaving at least a foot of overhang at the pond rim.

Pour pea gravel or smooth stones onto the shelf to create a gentle slope toward the pond bank. Lift the liner at the top and mound earth underneath to create a slightly higher grade than the pond rim. This prevents erosion of the beach by rain.

Soil can then be placed on the gravel above the waterline, and mulch placed over the liner edge. Pea gravel is a good planting medium for marginals such as arrowhead, cardinal flower and zebra rush. Smooth river rocks and boulders can be placed here and there on the pea gravel, as they might appear on a northern shore.

WHAT *about*
a BOG GARDEN?

W hat is a bog? When it comes to separating one damp place from another,
confused gardeners often tend to be less than specific. But nature is never vague
in differentiating wetland habitats.

BOGS

A bog is a nutrient-poor, acidic wetland that derives its water from rainfall. The surface layer is sphagnum moss (hence the term "peat bog") and is often quite dry and spongy.

❧ True bog plants are acid-loving and include native species such as highbush blueberry (*Vaccinium corymbosum*), Labrador tea (*Ledum groenlandicum*), bog laurel (*Kalmia polifolia*) and cranberry (*Vaccinium oxycoccum*). Trees might include tamarack, black spruce (*Picea mariana*) and swamp birch (*Betula pumila*).

❧ Many bog plants are evergreen to permit year-round photosynthesis; some, like pitcher plant (*Sarracenia purpurea*), rely on insects, rather than soil, for their nutrients.

A bog garden planted with delicate pink astilbe and stately Japanese iris makes a lovely counterpoint to this quiet pond.

Although there is no pond in this damp ravine, Japanese iris, yellow loosestrife and red astilbe thrive in the rich, marshy soil.

FENS

A fen receives its water from precipitation and from groundwater discharge such as that from an underground spring. A natural spring-fed country pond is, in scientific terms, a fen.

MARSHES

A marsh is a nutrient-rich wetland (freshwater or saltwater) that relies on precipitation and surface runoff from streams, rivers, ponds and lakes. Marshes generally have some standing water on a permanent basis,

but marsh plants are those adapted to seasonal changes in moisture levels — high in spring and fall and lower in summer.

❧ Common marsh plants include horsetail, cattail, arrowhead, spike rush, bulrush, bog arum, sweet flag, blue flag and great blue lobelia.

SWAMPS

There are two kinds — shrub swamps and tree swamps. A swamp receives its water and nutrients via overland flows from a river or nearby lake, or from ground sources such as springs. It might have

standing water most of the year, or become relatively dry in summer.

❧ Common plants found in swamps include red osier dogwood, willow, buttonbush, white cedar, tamarack, balsam fir, red maple, silver maple and black ash.

So, although we might refer to a damp garden as a "bog garden," in reality it is a freshwater marsh garden filled with native or non-native plants that are indigenous to wet meadows or to the marshy soil beside rivers, lakes and streams. And this is what you should be aiming for when you create a bog garden beside your pond.

Making *a* Bog Garden

A bog garden can be made adjacent to a pond to utilize the overflow caused by rain, or simply to soften the pond's edges, enhancing it with the type of landscape that might naturally occur beside a body of water. A bog garden can also be built independently of a pond — to exploit an area with poor drainage, or contrived artificially for the sole purpose of growing moisture-loving plants.

❧ Dig the area out to between 16 and 18 inches (40 to 45 cm) deep, removing the sod and topsoil to a tarp or plastic sheet, and the subsoil to the compost or to a waterfall construction, if that is part of the pond project. If the bog excavation is root-filled or very rocky, it may be advisable to line the excavation with geotextile before laying down a sheet of 30- to 40-mil PVC or 45-mil EPDM pond liner. (You can also use a rigid fiberglass pond shell, its bottom punctured for drainage, as a small bog garden.)

❧ If you're building the bog garden in conjunction with a pond, you may wish to extend the liner directly from the pond into the bog excavation. Keep the pond edging higher than the bog (use a boulder or concrete block underneath it, if necessary) to prevent backflow of the bog soil into the pond. Use a pitchfork to poke holes every 6 inches or so in the liner bottom.

❧ Fill the lined excavation with the sod, turned upside down, followed by the reserved topsoil amended in a 1:1 ratio with humus, to a depth of between 1 and 2 inches (2.5 to 5 cm) from the original soil level. Compost and leaf mold make good humus, but the easiest and cheapest humus for a bog garden is peat moss, thoroughly moistened with warm water. Peat moss is acidic, but most moisture-loving plants tend to like acid soils.

❧ If the soil remains very mucky, you may need to incorporate some sand or to poke a few more holes in the liner bottom. If the soil is very dry, you will need to water the garden on a frequent basis or install a simple drip irrigation system or a soaker hose. Another possible remedy for a bog garden that dries too quickly is to incorporate water-retaining polymer crystals in the soil. The garden should also be well mulched to prevent evaporation in periods of drought.

❧ Plant the bog garden with your favorite moisture-loving plants (see list, p. 65). Very wet areas in a bog garden can be planted with hardy emergent or marginal pond plants recommended for planting at water level (see Plants for Ponds, p. 77).

Japanese primroses thrive in the damp soil of a pond (below).

MOISTURE-LOVING PLANTS *for* BOG GARDENS *and* WATERSIDE

PERENNIALS *and* HARDY BULBS

- Astilbe (*Astilbe* spp.)
- Astrantia or masterwort (*A. major*)
- Beebalm or bergamot (*Monarda* spp.)
- Bergenia (*B. cordifolia*)
- Bugleweed (*Ajuga reptans*)
- Butterbur (*Petasites japonicus*)
- Camassia (*C. cusickii*)
- Canada anemone (*A. canadensis*)
- Canadian burnet (*Sanguisorba canadensis*)
- Candelabra primroses (*Primula beesiana, P. bulleyana, P. japonica, P pulverulenta,* Bullesiana hybrids)
- Cardinal flower (*Lobelia cardinalis*)
- Cow parsnip or giant hogweed (*Heracleum mantegazzianum*)
- Daylily (*Hemerocallis* spp.)
- European meadowsweet (*Filipendula ulmaria*)
- False Solomon's Seal (*Smilacina racemosa*)
- Globeflower (*Trollius* spp.)
- Goatsbeard (*Aruncus* spp.)
- Gooseneck loosestrife (*Lysimachia clethroides*)
- Great blue lobelia (*L. siphilitica*)
- Gunnera (*G. manicata*)
- Hosta (*Hosta* spp.)
- Ironweed (*Vernonia noveboracensis*)
- Japanese anemone (*A. X hybrida*)
- Japanese iris (*I. ensata*)
- Joe Pyeweed (*Eupatorium purpureum*)
- Knotweed (*Polygonum bistorta*)
- Lady's-mantle (*Alchemilla mollis*)
- Ligularia (*L. dentata*)
- Maiden grass (*Miscanthus* spp.)
- Marsh marigold (*Caltha palustris*)
- Monkey flower (*Mimulus guttatus*)
- Monkshood (*Aconitum* spp.)
- Obedient plant (*Physostegia virginiana*)
- Ornamental rhubarb (*Rheum palmatum*)
- Queen-of-the-prairie (*Filipendula rubra*)
- Rodgersia (*Rodgersia* spp.)
- Siberian bugloss (*Brunnera macrophylla*)
- Siberian iris (*I. sibirica*)
- Siebold primrose (*Primula sieboldii*)
- Skunk cabbage (*Lysichiton americanus*)
- Snakeroot or bugbane (*Cimicifuga racemosa*)
- Sneezeweed (*Helenium autumnale*)
- Spiderwort (*Tradescantia virginiana*)
- Summer snowflake (*Leucojum aestivum*)
- Swamp lily (*Lilium superbum*)
- Swamp milkweed (*Asclepias incarnata*)
- Swamp rose mallow (*Hibiscus moscheutos*)
- Turtlehead (*Chelone glabra*)
- Yellow flag iris (*I. pseudacorus*)
- Yellow loosestrife (*Lysimachia punctata*)

SHRUBS

- Arrowwood (*Viburnum dentatum*)
- Black willow (*Salix nigra*)
- Bog rosemary (*Andromeda polifolia*)
- Buttonbush (*Cephalanatus occidentalis*)
- Chokeberry (*Aronia melanocarpa; A. arbutifolia*)
- Downy or silky dogwood (*Cornus amomum*)
- Elderberry (*Sanguinaria canadensis*)
- Flowering raspberry (*Rubus odoratus*)
- Inkberry (*Ilex glabra*)
- Meadowsweet (*Spiraea latifolia*)
- Nannyberry (*Viburnum lentago*)
- Ninebark (*Physocarpus opulifolius*)
- Pussy willow (*Salix discolor*)
- Red osier dogwood (*Cornus stolonifera*)
- Serviceberry (*Amelanchier canadensis*)
- Summersweet (*Clethra alnifolia*)
- Swamp azalea (*Rhododendron viscosum*)
- Sweetspire (*Itea virginica*)
- Tatarian dogwood (*Cornus alba*)
- Winterberry (*Ilex verticillata*)
- Witherod viburnum (*V. cassinoides*)
- Yellow-stem dogwood (*Cornus stolonifera* 'Flavamirea')

FERNS

- Cinnamon fern (*Osmunda cinnamomea*)
- Goldie's wood fern (*Dryopteris goldiana*)
- Interrupted fern (*Osmunda claytoniana*)
- Lady fern (*Athyrium felix femina*)
- Ostrich fern (*Matteuccia struthiopteris*)
- Royal fern (*Osmunda regalis*)
- Sensitive fern (*Onoclea sensibilis*)

◀ *Japanese Iris* (I. ensata)

CHAPTER SIX

STOCKING
the POND

*P*lants and fish
transform a pool of still water into a vital
and exciting natural community — and a simple
garden into a work of water art.

POND PLANTS

There are four forms of aquatic plants that actually spend their lives (or, if tender or tropical, the growing season) in the water, under it, or floating on its surface:

Surfacing plants (e.g., water lily, lotus, floating heart), with leaves and flowers on or just above the water surface and roots planted either in a container of soil underwater, or directly in earth at the pond bottom. They derive their nutrients from the soil in which they're planted.

Free-floating plants (e.g., duckweed, water hyacinth, water lettuce) have leaves that float on the pond surface and unanchored roots that derive nutrients from the water itself.

Submerged oxygenating plants (e.g., hornwort, elodea), which spend their lives underwater performing two vital functions — utilizing nutrients that would otherwise feed algae, and providing oxygen-rich water for fish.

Marginal or emergent plants (e.g., arrowhead, sweet flag, papyrus) are those adapted to the edges or margins of the pond, with foliage that emerges from the water. They are planted either in pots that sit on underwater shelves or on blocks on the pond bottom, or are planted directly in soil basins in the pond bottom or, in a natural pond, in the muddy shallows at the shore. The shallowest marginal plants enjoy having their roots under water as long as their crowns rise above it, while deeper marginals are adapted to growing in water

Planting shelves accommodate marginal plants that need shallow water, while bricks or cinder blocks can be used under the pots of flowering aquatics to lift them to their optimal depth.

ranging in depth from a few inches to more than a foot.

❧ Water lilies (*Nymphaea* spp.) are the quintessential pond ornamentals and thrive with very little care — provided they're planted in rich heavy soil, receive lots of sun and have their dead flowers and foliage removed. There are diminutive water lilies small enough to be planted in patio pots; fuss-free hardy varieties in a rainbow of colors from white, pink and yellow to carmine and rich apricot; tender tropicals that take the color spectrum into blue and violet; and a few that wait until night to lift their exotic, perfumed blooms high above the water. (For cultivation information, see p. 70.)

❧ If you live in an area that enjoys long, hot summers, you can try your luck with the holy grail of water gardeners, the enchanting sacred lotus (*Nelumbo nucifera*) and its many hardy cultivars — hardy to Zone 6, if planted deep enough. With colorful blooms rising high out of the water and unusual seedpods so prized by flower arrangers, lotuses are a water-garden treasure.

❧ Then there are the water irises that lend a grace note to the shallows, from the shimmering lavender-blue *Iris versicolor* to the rich clear yellow of stately *I. pseudacorus*.

❧ No natural pond is complete without at least one native marginal — perhaps pickerel weed, with its tall spikes of intense blue, or arrowhead, whose potato-like tubers were once an important food for aboriginal people. And for those who have the space (and the will to prevent them from taking over), there are the twin tyrants of natural ponds — cattails and bulrushes.

HARDINESS *of* AQUATIC PLANTS

The degree of hardiness of many of the plants listed in this chapter varies considerably — depending on the depth of water in which they're planted and whether they're in containers or planted directly in soil in the pond bottom, where freezing may not occur as readily.

❧ Making the pond deeper by a foot and adding a foot of soil on top of the liner may allow you to successfully overwinter many plants that otherwise need protection.

❧ In tests conducted at Edmonton's Devonian Botanic Gardens (Zone 3), the hardy lilies 'Comanche', 'Escarboucle', 'Fabiola', 'Splendida' and 'Virginalis' survived consecutive winters planted in an earth-bottom pond at a depth of 4 feet (1.1 m). While such deep planting means it might take two seasons for the tubers to gain the size and strength to flower well, it is useful information for cold-climate water gardeners.

❧ Marginal plants that overwintered successive years at the Devonian in up to 2 feet (60 cm) of water include zebra rush, bog arum, arrowhead, narrow-leaf cattail, variegated cattail, yellow pond lily and yellow flag iris.

❧ But keeping things looking good on top of the water is only possible if all is well below. Oxygenating plants are the pond's true workhorses, absorbing dissolved nutrients that feed algae growth and supplying oxygen for fish to breathe, while providing shelter and spawning habitat in their dense foliage.

The following selection of aquatic plants is not complete by any means, but contains a variety of the above four categories of plants. Planting depth for marginals is approximate; many adapt to a wide range of water depths.

Water Lilies
(*Nymphaea* spp.)

There are more than 35 species of water lilies, most native to tropical or subtropical zones, with only a few hardy species native to temperate zones. Tropical water lilies have larger leaves and more colorful flowers than hardy species, and include some night-blooming varieties. However, hardy species have been crossed with tropicals to produce beautifully colored hardy water lily hybrids. Some tropical lilies are "viviparous," meaning they produce baby plants on their leaves.

HOW TO PLANT *a* WATER LILY

Do not plant lilies in turbulent water, or where they will be splashed by a waterfall or fountain — moving water prevents flower formation. Use of chemical algicides is also not recommended near water lilies.

STEP 1

❧ At nurseries, water lilies are sold in pots; mail-order plants are delivered with bare roots (and with fewer roots than the lily pictured at left, photographed at the end of a full season of growth). They should be transplanted to large pots (at least a half-bushel container) to allow their roots to grow.

STEP 2

❧ Choose round or square mesh containers made for pond plants, with openings in their sides. These allow the fine roots of plants to grow through the sides but don't let soil escape. Containers with larger holes should be lined with burlap to hold the soil. Half-fill the basket with heavy garden soil (no peat moss or compost) or specially formulated aquatic plant soil.

STEP 3

❧ Remove the water lily from its pot, gently spread the roots and set it firmly on the soil, allowing its crown to sit well above the surface.

❧ Tropical water lily tubers are planted almost vertically. Most hardy water lily rhizomes are planted at a 45° angle, with the exception of hardy *Nymphaea odorata* hybrids (marked with * on our plant list, p. 74), which are planted horizontally. Odorata hybrids are fast-growing, and require a very large planting container. With hardy water lilies, always place the cut end of the rhizome against the wall of the pot so the rhizome has more room to grow.

❧ Water the soil and allow it to settle. Add more soil over the roots and around the crown. The crown

The first hardy water lily hybrids were developed by the French breeder, Marliac, in the late 19th century; many of his crosses continue to be popular today. One of the foremost tropical hybridizers was George Pring of Missouri, and many popular tropicals bear his patent name.

All water lilies need full sun (6 hours) and warm water for maximum flower production. Hardy lilies are planted from late April to June, when the water temperature has reached 15°C (60°F). Colder water may stunt growth. Tropicals need a starting temperature of 20°C (70°F) and are planted in May or June, depending on climate zone. But tropicals will continue flowering into early autumn, depending on water temperatures, well after hardy lilies have gone dormant.

Hardy and tropical water lilies are heavy feeders, requiring rich heavy soil. Supplemental fertilizer can take the form of special aquatic organic fertilizer, fertilizer tablets or slow-release fertilizer briquettes especially formulated for aquatic plants and used only once per season. Hardy water lilies must be divided every 1 to 3 years to retain their vigor.

Water lilies make excellent cut flowers. Conditioned well, they can last 4 to 5 days; leave the cut flowers floating in the sun for 30 minutes, then use a dab of wax or nail polish on the base of each petal to prevent it from closing.

pea gravel to a depth of at least 1 inch (2.5 cm). The gravel holds the soil in the basket, protects the crown and prevents soil from washing over it.

STEP 5

❧ Carefully lower the basket into the pond. To achieve the right height, set containers on bricks or pavers on the bottom of the pond.

❧ The type of water lily will dictate the depth of planting: from 2 to

should remain just above the surface — soil in the crown can prevent good growth. Water again, allowing the soil to settle; check to be sure the crown is still at the right level.

❧ If the soil is rich, fertilizing at planting time is not essential. If desired, push 3 fertilizer tablets, such as *Sera* or *Pondtabbs*, a couple of inches (5 cm) into the soil.

STEP 4

❧ When the second watering has completely settled and the position of the crown has been checked and adjusted, cover the soil surface with

4 inches (5 to 10 cm) of water above the crown for the tropical blue-flowered *Nymphaea colorata*, to 3 feet (1 m) or more for the hardy white cultivar, 'Gladstone'. Because water near the surface of the pond is warmer than deep water, tropical hybrids are generally planted with 4 inches (10 cm) of water over the crown for the first month, then lowered to between 6 and 8 inches (15 to 20 cm). For correct planting depth for individual lilies, check with your water-garden supplier.

Hardy water lilies are not bothered by many pests but can be susceptible to a fungal disease called crown rot, in which the rhizome becomes mushy, foliage is sparsely produced and turns yellow soon after unfolding, and flower buds rot and fall before opening. Since crown rot is difficult to combat and is highly contagious, it's best to buy your hardy lilies from a reputable dealer, preferably one who grows his or her own nursery stock.

Insect pests include water lily beetles and plum aphid. Use a hose to wash them off the leaves into the pond, where they make a tasty meal for fish.

Overwintering Water Lilies

HARDY VARIETIES

❧ Hardy water lilies may be overwintered in their containers in the pond, provided the roots do not freeze solid. If the pond has a deep zone where water does not freeze — from 2.5 to 6 feet (0.8 to 2 m), depending on the frost line in your area — the container should be moved there.

❧ Alternatively, lilies can be lifted in their containers before freeze-up and, after their foliage has been removed, they can be stored in a cool cellar or garage (5 to 10°C/40 to 50°F) for the winter. Do not let rhizomes dry out. In spring, new growth will appear and lilies can be put back in the pond, or removed from the pot and divided, if tubers have become crowded.

TROPICAL VARIETIES

❧ Tropicals are usually treated as (rather expensive) annuals. Although overwintering can be attempted in the same way that hardy lilies are treated, the outcome is not guaranteed.

❧ Alternatively, you can wait until the pond water has cooled to 10°C (50°F), then bring the lily in its container into a cool basement or garage. Remove the plant from the pot and rinse off the dirt, then allow it to air-dry for 2 to 3 days before cutting off the leaves and stems.

❧ Separate the tubers (new ones may have formed) and place them in lukewarm water for 24 hours. Check the condition of the submerged tubers — those that sank can be saved, while the others should be discarded.

❧ Air-dry the retained tubers in a cool room for a few days, then place them in the middle of cool, damp (not wet) sand in a plastic bag. Store the closed bag at 13°C (55°F) until four weeks before the last frost date in your area.

❧ If the tubers have sprouted, place each in a 5-inch (12 cm) pot, barely covering it with heavy topsoil, then with a layer of pebbles. If not, place them in water on a sunny windowsill to sprout.

❧ Place pots with sprouted tubers in a tub or fish tank and cover with water heated to between 20 and 22°C (70 to 74°F). Use an aquarium heater to heat the water. When new growth begins, the tubers should be moved to a well-lit area, or fluorescent lights can be set up over the tank.

❧ When the pond has warmed to 20°C (70°F), the tubers can be transplanted in fresh soil in containers and returned to their summer home.

Unless hardy water lilies can be moved to deep water where their rhizomes will not freeze in winter, they should be lifted in autumn and stored in a cool place indoors.

Hardy Water Lilies

With a small spread (4 to 5 square feet) and suitable for tubs or small ponds

PINK
- ❧ 'Pink Opal'
- ❧ 'Joanne Pring'

WHITE
- ❧ *N. odorata pumila* * (Zone 4)
- ❧ *N. tetragona* (Zone 3)
- ❧ 'Candida'

YELLOW
- ❧ 'Pygmaea Helvola' (very tiny)

CHANGEABLE
- ❧ 'Aurora'
- ❧ 'Graziella'
- ❧ 'Indiana'
- ❧ 'Little Sue'
- ❧ 'Paul Harriot'

With a medium-large spread (6 to 10 square feet)

PINK
- ❧ 'Arc en Ciel' *
- ❧ 'Fabiola'
- ❧ 'Gloire de temple sur Lot'
- ❧ 'Hollandia'
- ❧ 'Marliac Carnea'
- ❧ 'Marliac Rose'
- ❧ 'Mary'
- ❧ 'Masaniello'
- ❧ 'Nigel'
- ❧ 'Norma Gedye'
- ❧ 'Pearl of the Pool' *
- ❧ 'Pink Pumpkin'
- ❧ 'Pink Sensation'
- ❧ 'Pink Sunrise'
- ❧ 'Rose Arey'
- ❧ 'Yuh Ling'

RED
- ❧ 'Burgundy Princess'
- ❧ 'Gloriosa'
- ❧ 'James Brydon'
- ❧ 'Laydekeri Fulgens' (or smaller)
- ❧ 'Liou' (or smaller)
- ❧ 'Mayla'
- ❧ 'Red Spider'

WHITE
- ❧ 'Gonnere'
- ❧ 'Hal Miller'
- ❧ 'Hermine'
- ❧ 'Marliac White'
- ❧ 'Mme. Julien Chifflot'
- ❧ 'Virginalis'

YELLOW
- ❧ 'Charlene Strawn'
- ❧ 'Chromatella'
- ❧ 'Moorei'
- ❧ 'Lemon Chiffon'

CHANGEABLE
- ❧ 'Sioux'

With a large spread (10 to 12 square feet)

PINK
- ❧ 'Amabilis'
- ❧ 'Firecrest'

RED
- ❧ 'Attraction'
- ❧ 'Charles de Meurville'
- ❧ 'Escarboucle'
- ❧ 'Rembrandt'
- ❧ 'Sultan'

WHITE
- ❧ *Nymphaea alba* (Zone 6)
- ❧ *Nymphaea odorata* * (Zone 4)
- ❧ 'Gladstone'

YELLOW
- ❧ 'Sunrise'

CHANGEABLE
- ❧ 'Comanche'

Tropical Water Lilies

Day-blooming, with a small spread (3 to 4 square feet)

BLUE
- ❧ *Nymphaea colorata*
- ❧ 'Dauben'

Day-blooming, with a medium-large spread (8 to 16 square feet)

PINK/RED
- ❧ 'Castelliflora'
- ❧ 'General Pershing'
- ❧ 'Jack Ward'
- ❧ 'Madame Ganna Walska'
- ❧ 'Pink Capensis'
- ❧ 'Pink Pearl'
- ❧ 'Pink Platter'

WHITE
- ❧ 'Crystal'
- ❧ 'Marion Strawn' (or smaller)

BLUE/PURPLE/VIOLET
- ❧ 'August Koch'
- ❧ 'Blue Star' (or smaller)
- ❧ 'Blue Triumph Hybrid'
- ❧ 'Director Moore'
- ❧ 'Electra'
- ❧ 'King of the Blues'
- ❧ 'Marmota'
- ❧ 'Mrs. Martin Randig'
- ❧ 'Midnight'
- ❧ 'Nora'
- ❧ 'Panama Pacific'
- ❧ 'Tina'

YELLOW
- ❧ 'St. Louis Gold' (or smaller)

APRICOT
- ❧ 'Albert Greenberg'
- ❧ 'Golden West'

GREEN
- ❧ 'Green Smoke'

Day-blooming, with a large spread (16 to 25 square feet)

PINK/RED
- ❧ 'Mrs. C.W. Ward'

WHITE
- ❧ 'Mrs. George H. Pring'
- ❧ 'White Delight'

BLUE/PURPLE/VIOLET
- ❧ 'Blue Beauty'
- ❧ 'William Stone'

YELLOW
- ❧ 'Yellow Dazzler'

Night-blooming, with a medium-large spread (8 to 16 square feet)

PINK/RED
- ❧ 'Emily Grant Hutchings'
- ❧ 'Red Cup'
- ❧ 'Red Flare'
- ❧ 'Sturtevanti'
- ❧ 'Texas Shell Pink'

WHITE
- ❧ 'Wood's White Night'

Night-blooming, with a large spread (16 to 25 square feet)

PINK/RED
- ❧ 'Mrs. George C. Hitchcock'
- ❧ 'Maroon Beauty'
- ❧ 'Rubra'

WHITE
- ❧ 'Missouri'
- ❧ 'Sir Galahad'

* *Nymphaea odorata* hybrids — plant rhizomes horizontally

PLANTS FOR PONDS *and* POOLS

Lotuses (*Nelumbo* spp.)

SACRED LOTUS
(*Nelumbo nucifera*)

❀ Native to the Orient, this sacred flower of the Hindu religion has been in cultivation for at least 2,500 years. Leaves can reach between 1 and 2 feet (30 to 60 cm) in length and often rise on strong stems more than 4 feet (1.3 m) above the water. Flowers are often fragrant, large (to 12 inches/30 cm), either white or pink (*N. nucifera speciosum*) and look like huge roses. They develop distinctive seedheads which look like shower nozzles and are often used in dried arrangements. Seed is viable for hundreds of years.

❀ Plant banana-shape tubers horizontally 2 inches (5 cm) deep in rich soil in a very large planting container, taking care not to damage the fragile growing tip which should just poke out of the soil. Start under 4 to 6 inches (10 to 15 cm) of water at first, lowering to 12 inches (30 cm) as plants develop. Slow to establish, only leaves may develop the first year.

❀ Sacred lotus and its cultivars require many weeks of warm, sunny weather to flower. Cultivars can be winter-hardy to Zone 6, especially if planted in an earth-bottom pond or in containers in water deep enough so crown and tuber do not freeze. Winter care is the same as that of hardy water lilies.

Sacred Lotus (Nelumbo nucifera)

CULTIVARS

❀ 'CHAWAN BASU' — delicate, pink-edged white flowers. Prolific. Good for small ponds and tubs.

❀ 'MAGGIE BELLE SLOCUM' — magenta blooms with petals folded like quills. Adapts to ponds and small tubs.

❀ 'MOMO BATAN' — double dark rose flowers, a little like a peony on small plants. Suitable for a small pond or tub culture.

❀ 'MRS. PERRY SLOCUM' — huge flowers (often 12 inches/30 cm) that open deep pink, take on yellow tones the second day and turn creamy yellow-pink by the third.

❀ 'PERRY'S GIANT SUNBURST' — huge, elegant flowers of pale sulphur-yellow.

YELLOW AMERICAN LOTUS
(*Nelumbo lutea*)

❀ Native from southern Ontario into the southern United States. Large, round, blue-green leaves and 10-inch (25 cm) pale yellow flowers are both held high above the water. Hardier than sacred lotus and used in cross-breeding with that tender species. Needs rich soil and warm temperatures to flower. Zone 6.

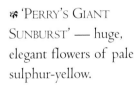

POND LILIES
(*Nuphar* spp.)

❧ Pond lilies are best in very large, earth-bottom ponds. Their aggressive root systems make container planting difficult at best.

❧ YELLOW POND LILY (*Nuphar advena*) — very hardy North American native, with heart-shape leaves and small, yellow tulip-like flowers. Needs some sun to flower well. Zone 5.

❧ YELLOW WATER LILY (*Nuphar lutea*) — yellow buttercup-like flowers. Prefers deep (6 feet/2 m), somewhat acidic, often moving, water. Vigorous. Zone 5.

Oxygenating Plants

❧ CANADIAN PONDWEED, WATERWEED (*Elodea canadensis*) — hardy native North American, with branched stems and lacy whorled leaves. May be rooted in soil or pea gravel, or used as free-floating cuttings. Leaves are eaten by goldfish and used as habitat for fish fry. Excellent oxygenator but can be invasive in natural, clay-bottom ponds. Zone 4.

❧ HORNWORT (*Ceratophyllum demersum*) — very hardy native North American that grows entirely submerged, bearing branched stems with whorls of fine, bristle-like leaves. Tolerant of cold, deep water (to 30 feet/10 m), but also an excellent shallow-pond oxygenator and habitat for fish spawn and fry. Best and easiest oxygenator to use because it doesn't require a pot — cuttings can simply be dropped into the water. Zone 5.

❧ RIBBON GRASS OR EEL GRASS (*Vallisneria americana*) — North American native, sometimes called wild celery, with light-green ribbon-shape leaves. Grows to 24 inches (60 cm). Popular food for ducks and waterfowl. Requires planting in soil; cuttings can be easily rooted. Tender.

Free-Floating Aquatic Plants

❧ DUCKWEED (*Lemna minor*) — a true aquatic fern, with small leaves and no flowers. It multiplies quickly to shade pond and control algae. Good fish food. Sometimes appears in ponds without being planted, since it is carried on the feathers of ducks. Invasive. Zone 5.

❧ FAIRY MOSS (*Azolla caroliniana*) — fuzzy floating carpet of tiny, fern-like plants. Green in summer, but turns crimson in cool weather. Frost-tender but might be overwintered indoors in a stock pan of pond soil and water.

❧ FROG'S BIT (*Hydrocharis morsus-ranae*) — small white flowers in spring and round floating leaves. Stolons spread horizontally, making tiny new plants at their ends. In natural ponds, new plants drop to the bottom in fall, then sprout the next spring and rise to the surface again. Invasive. Zone 5.

❧ WATER FERN OR WATER VELVET (*Salvinia rotundifolia*) — aquatic fern with small, hairy floating leaves that appear dry, even after being submerged. Shade tolerant. Aggressive. Tender.

❧ WATER HYACINTH (*Eichornia crassipes major*) — very popular floating aquatic with spongy air-filled leaves and attractive purple

Water Hyacinth (Eichornia crassipes major)

flowers marked with yellow. Very long trailing roots provide spawning habitat for fish and deprive algae of nutrients. Used industrially to purify polluted water. Flowering is often sparse, which may be due to the roots being eaten by fish, so netting protector is advisable. Flowering also improves when roots anchor, rather than float unattached. Frost-tender but might overwinter in moist soil in a greenhouse or sunroom.

❧ WATER LETTUCE (*Pistia stratiotes*) — no flowers but attractive rosettes of blue-green leaves. Good plant for fish spawning and protection, and an excellent shade plant to control algae. Use netting protector to deter browsing koi. Tender, but may overwinter in a greenhouse or sunroom aquarium.

❦ WATER MEAL (*Wolffia* spp.) — very tiny aquatic fern that looks like surface algae. Smallest free-floater, fast to multiply, but easily scooped out. Tender.

❦ WATER POPPY (*Hydrocleyes nymphoides*) — a profusion of yellow poppy-like flowers held above glossy leaves. Excellent for small ponds and tubs. Tender.

Water Poppy (Hydrocleyes nymphoides)

Hardy Marginal (or Emergent) Aquatic Plants

Emergent or marginal plants are those that survive with roots or lower stems submerged in varying depths of water on a permanent basis. Those planted at water level may also thrive in the moist soil of a bog. (See Plants for Bog Gardens, p. 65.)

For Planting *at* Water Level

❦ ALLEGHENY MONKEY FLOWER (*Mimulus ringens*) — native from Nova Scotia to Manitoba. 1 to 2 feet (30 to 60 cm) high, with violet-blue flowers. Zone 4.

❦ ARROW ARUM (*Peltandra virginica*) — native plant bearing long, shiny, arrow-shape leaves and inconspicuous green flowers in May-June; may be followed by green berries. Grows to 3 feet (1 m). Zone 6.

❦ BOG ARUM (*Calla palustris*) — small calla-type bloom of white spathe surrounding a yellow spadix in spring which, if pollinated by pond snails, produces red berries. Needs quiet water. Grows 9 to 12 inches (22 to 30 cm) tall. Zone 5.

❦ CARDINAL FLOWER (*Lobelia cardinalis*) — beautiful native with deep red flowers on 3- to 4-foot (1 to 1.3 m) spikes. Attracts hummingbirds. Likes part shade and wet soil near streams. Adapts to deeper standing water. Lowering crown under water in fall might prevent death of plant in winter. Good bog plant. Zone 4.

Cardinal Flower (Lobelia cardinalis)

❦ GREAT BLUE LOBELIA (*L. siphilitica*) — this native blooms from August to September, with vivid blue-purple flower spikes on 2- to 3-foot (60 to 90 cm) stems. Tolerant of standing water. Best when divided every few years. Zone 6.

❦ HOUTTUYNIA (*H. cordata*) — sometimes called chameleon plant because of its striking green/red variegated foliage and white flowers. Also used as damp-border perennial. Grows 6 to 12 inches (15 to 30 cm) high. Invasive. Zone 6.

Marsh Marigold (Caltha palustris)

❦ MARSH MARIGOLD (*Caltha palustris*) — very adaptable native, with kidney-shape leaves and bright yellow buttercup-like flowers in early spring. Foliage sometimes disappears in summer and reappears in fall. Grows 9 to 15 inches (22 to 38 cm) tall. Beautiful paired with water forget-me-not. Double-flowered form is *C. palustris* 'Plena'. White form is *C. p.* 'Alba'. Zone 4.

❦ MICRO-MINIATURE CATTAIL (*Typha minima*) — better behaved than other cattails, this Japanese species grows 1 to 2 feet (30 to 60 cm) tall. Good for small ponds. Zone 6.

❦ SWAMP MILKWEED (*Asclepias incarnata*) — along with dry-land milkweeds, this native plant is the larval food for the monarch butterfly. Dull pink summer flower clusters. Grows 3 to 5 feet (90 to 150 cm) high. Good bog plant. Zone 4.

❧ VARIEGATED MANNA GRASS (*Glyceria aquatica* 'Variegata') — good foliage plant, with green, white and yellow striped leaves. Grows 18 to 24 inches (45 to 60 cm) tall. Zone 5.

❧ WATER FORGET-ME-NOT (*Myosotis palustris* or *M. scorpiodes*) — clambering stems and bright blue yellow-centered flowers, much like biennial forget-me-not, but blooms later and over a long period of time. Good in bogs. Zone 6.

Water Forget-Me-Not (Myosotis palustris)

For Planting 2 Inches (4 cm) Deep

❧ ARROWHEAD (*Sagittaria latifolia*) — this native has grass-like foliage when young, then develops typical arrowhead leaves. Tall spikes of delicate white flowers grow to 2 feet (60 cm). Good for protecting pond banks against erosion. Double arrowhead is *S. japonica* 'Flore Pleno', with beautiful double, white, carnation-like flowers. Zone 6.

Arrowhead (Sagittaria latifolia)

❧ BLUE WATER IRIS OR BLUE FLAG (*I. versicolor*) — native that blooms in May and June, with several blue-violet flowers on 18- to 24-inch (45 to 60 cm) stems. Zone 4.

❧ CATTAIL (*Typha latifolia*) — a common sight in marshes, ditches and pond margins where conditions range from wet soil to several feet of standing water. Velvety brown pokers

Cattail (Typha latifolia)

have separated male and female flower segments. Grows to height of between 6 and 9 feet (2 to 3 m). Creeping rhizomes are highly invasive — must be planted in containers. Zone 4.

❧ CORKSCREW RUSH (*Juncus effusus* 'Spiralis') — interesting spiral shape to the stems of this native rush, which grows to 18 inches (45 cm). Confine roots to a container to prevent spreading. Good in flower arrangements. Zone 5.

❧ DWARF CATTAIL (*Typha laxmanni*) — at 3 feet (1 m), this is a good short alternative to the tall common cattail, with the same brown summer catkins. Like all cattails, however, it is very invasive, so plant in a container. Zone 5.

❧ DWARF JAPANESE SWEET FLAG (*Acorus gramineus*) — from the arum family, this dainty grassy plant grows about 18 inches (45 cm) tall. There is an excellent, showy yellow-striped form, *A. gramineus* 'Variegatus'. Zone 5.

❧ GRACEFUL CATTAIL OR NARROW-LEAF CATTAIL (*Typha angustifolia*) — at 6 feet (2 m), still a tall cattail but its narrow, elegant foliage distinguishes it from the common variety. Restrain roots in containers to curb spreading. Do not remove foliage from any cattails (or bulrushes) until spring, to let plants breathe. Zone 4.

❧ FLOWERING RUSH (*Butomus umbellatus*) — one of the best flowering marginals, with 3- to 4-foot (1 to 1.3 m) stems bearing rose-pink flower umbels. Triangular, rush-like leaves start out burgundy, then turn rich green in summer. Zone 6.

❧ LIZARD'S TAIL OR WATER DRAGON (*Saururus cernuus*) — curled, fluffy, white flower spikes are fragrant, long-lasting in summer. Handsome, narrow leaves. Zone 6.

❧ PICKEREL RUSH OR PICKERELWEED (*Pontederia cordata*) — long heart-shape leaves and a profusion of intense blue flower spikes rising 2 to 3 feet (60 to 90 cm) from this native plant in mid-summer to fall. Fertilize to encourage continued flowering. Easily grown, and a must for pond gardeners. Zone 5.

Pickerel Rush (Pontederia cordata)

❧ PRIMROSE CREEPER (*Jussiaea diffusa*) — belongs to evening-primrose family. Creeping stems with bright-yellow 2-inch (5 cm) flowers. Shade tolerant. Zone 6.

❧ ROSE MALLOW OR WATER HIBISCUS (*Hibiscus moscheutos* or *H. palustris*) — native to fresh and saltwater marshes of Carolina, Massachusetts, and Florida west to Indiana. Huge pink, red and white hollyhock-like flowers on 6-foot (2 m) stems. Garden selection is *H. moscheutos* 'Southern Belle'. May not overwinter but will

Rose Mallow (Hibiscus moscheutos 'Southern Belle')

flower the first year from seed started indoors. Zone 7.

❧ SPIKE RUSH (*Eleocharis montevidensis*) — low, dense plant with quilled, rush-like leaves and brown spiky summer flowers. Height is about 8 to 12 inches (22 to 30 cm) but varies according to depth of planting. Zone 5.

❧ SWEET FLAG (*Acorus calamus*) — native to Asia but naturalized in North America. Leaves emit a sweet lemony scent. Sword-like foliage and textured gold flower spadix. Grows 2 to 4 feet (60 to 120 cm) tall. To prevent mildew, plant in full sun. Wear gloves when cutting; sweet flag has been known to cause a skin rash. Variegated form is *A. calamus* 'Variegatus'. Zone 4.

❧ WATER PLANTAIN (*Alisma plantago-aquatica*) — young foliage of this native plant is ribbon-like, but older ribbed leaves float on surface. Pale-pink flowers on 2- to 3-foot (60 to 90 cm) stems in summer. Flowers best in shallow water. Zone 5.

❧ YELLOW WATER IRIS (*I. pseudacorus*) — reliable and elegant to 4 feet (1.3 m), the big yellow spring flower of this naturalized European is the fleur-de-lys on the French coat of arms. Vigorous; will grow in shallow water or moist garden soil. Yellow-green variegated form is *I. pseudacorus* 'Variegata'. Zone 4.

For Planting 6 Inches (15 cm) Deep

❧ BOGBEAN (*Menyanthes trifoliata*) — very hardy native marsh plant that spreads by rhizomes. Bean-like leaves and fragrant, starry, white flowers with stems that creep over water. Good for disguising edges of artificial ponds. Zone 5.

❧ BULRUSH (*Scirpus validus*) — sometimes confused with cattail, but bears flat-topped spiky brown flowers, not catkins. This native sedge is common in sunny marshes and shallow water to 3 feet (1 m). Bulrushes are being tested as natural biological cleansers at industrial sites with contaminated run-off. Somewhat invasive, so best grown in container in pond. Zone 5.

❧ FLOATING HEART OR WATER FRINGE (*Nymphoides peltata*) — stoliniferous, with purple-mottled, round leaves and frilly yellow flowers rising 2 inches (5 cm) above

Floating Heart (Nymphoides peltata)

the water. Vigorous; needs periodic thinning. Will root in mud; tolerates depths up to 20 inches (50 cm). Good fish fry habitat. Zone 5.

Melon Sword (Echinodorus cordifolius)

❧ MELON SWORD (*Echinodorus cordifolius*) — native from Illinois to southern United States. Long, upright leaves; white flowers on whorled stems become prostrate on the water. Zone 6.

❧ SPEARWORT OR TONGUE BUTTERCUP (*Ranunculus lingua*) — stolon-forming aquatic buttercup, with erect stems bearing golden-yellow flowers from June to August. Adapts to water from 2 to 12 inches (5 to 30 cm) deep. Zone 5.

❧ WATER CLOVER, PEPPERWORT, WATER SHAMROCK (*Marsilea* spp.) — European and Asian aquatic fern that has naturalized and is hardy in parts of eastern North America. Four-part shamrock-like leaves float in 6- to 8-inch (15 to 20 cm) deep water, but will stand erect in shallower water. Zone 5.

❧ WHITE RUSH (*Scirpus lacustris* ssp. *tabernaemontani* 'Albescens') — pale green-and-yellow-striped bulrush, growing to 6 feet (2 m). Better for gardens than common bulrush. Zone 5.

❧ ZEBRA RUSH (*Scirpus lacustris* ssp. *tabernaemontani* 'Zebrinus') — quill-like stems, banded green and white, become greener as summer progresses. Grows 1 to 3 feet (30 to 90 cm) tall. Zone 6.

Zebra Rush (Scirpus lacustris *ssp.* tabernaemontani *'Zebrinus'*)

Tropical/Tender Marginal Aquatics

Most tropical aquatics are treated as annuals in garden ponds but a few, such as umbrella palm and papyrus, can be wintered indoors as houseplants.

For Planting *at* Water Level

❧ BOG LILY OR SWAMP LILY (*Crinum americanum*) — native to marshes and slow streams in southern United States. Has sweet-scented, spidery white flowers on 2-foot (60 cm) stems in July and August.

❧ GREEN TARO OR ELEPHANT'S EAR (*Colocasia escuelenta*) — grows to height of between 2 and 3 feet (60 to 90 cm), with yellow, rank-smelling arum flowers in hot summers.

❧ IMPERIAL TARO (*Colocasia antiquorum illustris*) — thick stems to 3-1/2 feet (105 cm) and dark-blotched long, oval leaves. Makes a good houseplant.

❧ MONKEY FLOWER OR MONKEY MUSK (*Mimulus guttatus*) — found from Mexico to Alaska. Showy yellow flowers; self-seeds prolifically and can be relied upon to return year after year, even in colder climates. Good in a bog.

❧ TROPICAL WATER CANNA (*C. aquatica*) — similar to garden canna. Large, elliptical leaves, with long-blooming orange-yellow flowers. Many good peach, red and pink cultivars.

❧ UMBRELLA PALM (*Cyperus alternifolius*) — very popular tropical aquatic in naturalistic ponds, and an excellent centerpiece in a formal pond. Stems bear palm-like umbels of spiky flowers. Grows about 2.5 feet (75 cm) tall, but taller forms are available. Dwarf form is *C. alternifolius gracilis* which, at 12 to 18 inches (30 to 45 cm) tall, is a good choice for a tub garden.

❧ WATER CANNA OR BLUE FIRE FLAG (*Thalia dealbata*) — native to southern United States. Long, narrow, blue-gray, canna-type leaves and spikes of small pale purple flowers on 4- to 5-foot (1.3 to 1.6 m) stems.

For Planting 2 Inches (4 cm) Deep

❧ DWARF PAPYRUS (*Cyperus haspan*) — one of the smaller umbrella sedges, growing 1 to 2 feet (30 to 60 cm) tall, with feathery reddish-brown spikelets.

Papyrus (Cyperus papyrus)

❧ PAPYRUS (*Cyperus papyrus*) — used by the ancient Egyptians as writing paper, and still used for mats and sandals. Mophead spikelets, triangular leaves on tall 4- to 8-foot (1.3 to 2.6 m) stems.

❧ SPIDER LILY (*Hymenocallis liriosme*) — native to sunny marshes in southern United States. Glossy, strap-shape foliage and 12-inch (30 cm) flower scapes bearing several white blossoms in summer.

❧ WATER PARSLEY (*Oenanthes sarmentosa*) — native to marshes from northern California to southern B.C.

For Planting *at* 6 Inches (15 cm) *or* Deeper

❧ GOLDEN CLUB (*Orontium aquaticum*) — a very striking plant, also called "never-wet" because leaves appear dry, even after being submerged. Unusual yellow poker flowers on white stems in spring. Grows 3 to 12 inches (8 to 30 cm) deep. Tubers may overwinter below frostline.

❧ PARROT'S FEATHER (*Myriophyllum proserpinacoides* or *M. brasiliense*) — light green plume-like leaves grow in whorls around 6- to 8-inch (15 to 20 cm) stems rising out of the water. Grown for its foliage, not for the inconspicuous white flowers. Tolerates shade and moving water, even waterfalls. Try overwintering cuttings in a cool stock pan. (NOTE: Eurasian or spiked water

Parrot's Feather
(Myriophyllum proserpinacoides)

milfoil, *M. spicatum*, is an invasive aquatic weed and should never be introduced into a natural pond.)

❧ WATER HAWTHORN (*Aponogeton distachyus*) — named for the nocturnal vanilla or hawthorn scent of the distinctive spiked flowers, which are white with black stamens. Thick, lustrous green leaves splotched with purple and brown. Flowers both in early spring and late fall, but not in summer heat. Can be planted between 1 and 4 feet (.3 to 1.3 m) deep.

White Water Snowflake
(Nymphoides cristatum)

❧ WHITE WATER SNOWFLAKE (*Nymphoides cristatum* or *N. indica*) — sweet little plant with floating leaves that resemble water lilies, and small erect flowers lasting one day. Free-flowering. May survive light frost.

❧ YELLOW WATER SNOWFLAKE (*Nymphoides geminata* or *N. germanica*) — small fringed yellow flowers and mottled leaves similar to white water snowflake.

GOLDFISH *and* KOI

No pond picture is complete without at least a few fish gliding through the depths — their glittering, scaled bodies reflecting the sunlight through the water, their flashing movements animating the serene tableau of water lilies and reflected sky.

Fish perform a useful function in a pond. They have a voracious appetite for insect larvae, particularly those of mosquitoes, which tend to breed in still water (less so in water disturbed by a fountain or bubbler), so they're the pond gardener's best friend.

While it's not possible to have too few fish, it is definitely dangerous to overstock a pond, particularly with big fish like koi, which eat large quantities of food and produce equivalent amounts of waste. (See A Short Course in Pond Ecology, p. 25.)

COMMON GOLDFISH

❦ These grow to about 6 inches (15 cm), with a squat body and a short tail. Goldfish prefer cold water, tolerating water temperatures from just above freezing to almost 30°C (86°F). They are a good beginner's fish — very easy to keep and requiring little in the way of extra food in a well-planted natural pond, where brown algae and water bugs will be plentiful. But if supplemental feedings are desired,

Brilliantly colored fish animate the pond scene.

the fish should be fed no more than what they will consume in 2 to 3 minutes.

❦ Related to the common goldfish are Comets and Shubunkins. Comets have longer bodies than the common species, are equally hardy and have beautiful coloration. They are very fast and graceful swimmers. Shubunkins have dull, mottled bodies with orange and white variations on a blue-tone skin.

FANCY GOLDFISH

❦ Fancy varieties — such as Orandas, Fantails, Lionheads, Fringetails, Black Moors and China Dolls — are not as hardy as common goldfish and their descendant strains, and need to be overwintered in an aquarium indoors. Many are not as fast or agile, leaving them prey to predators such as raccoons and cats.

GOLDEN ORFES

❦ These fish are surface feeders and can be seen streaking across the pond in schools; this trait demands that they be kept in quantity. They enjoy moving water, like that tumbling into the pond from a waterfall. Because of their fast swimming, active regimens and ultimate size (2 feet/60 cm), orfes are best in big, deep ponds.

KOI

❦ Koi are the aristocrats of the pond, treasured since antiquity by Japanese and Chinese water gardeners as individual personalities, with rare breeds and colors commanding astronomic prices among collectors. But because koi can reach more than 12 inches (30 cm) in length, with considerable weight, they are not a good choice for a small garden pond. To accommodate their need for exercise and their penchant for vertical swimming, they need a pond with a minimum length of 9 feet (3 m), longer if possible, and a water depth in some part of the pond of 3 to 5 feet (1 to 1.6 m).

❦ Because koi also tend to disturb the soil of aquatic plants, eating the roots of many and muddying the water, they are best isolated in their own ponds. Some water gardeners use this fact to advantage, making a deep koi pond whose water is pumped through a second shallow, densely planted pond that acts as a natural filter. Here, selected marginal aquatics remove impurities from the koi water before pumping it back into their pond. A well-balanced double pond system can reduce or eliminate the need for a biofilter.

POND PESTS

CATS

❦ Provided the pond is at least 18 inches (45 cm) deep and there are pots of water lilies and aquatics, preferably on supports so fish can swim underneath, cats rarely have luck catching fish. In winter, however, fish surface as the sun melts the pond ice, then become trapped when the ice freezes around them — making them easy prey for cats. Keep the pond netted if cats stalk fish during winter.

GEESE, DUCKS and WATERFOWL

❦ The shores of large, earth-bottom ponds are often frequented by waterfowl, especially Canada geese, that multiply rapidly and produce considerable excreta which, in turn, fouls the pond and causes algae.

❦ Geese and ducks are vegetarians and feed on ornamental aquatic plants. They prefer unplanted banks, which permit easy access to the water — so landscaping the edges with shrubs and perennials and planting the shallow areas deters waterfowl.

RACCOONS

❦ Raccoons are most likely to catch fish in very shallow fiberglass or polyethylene ponds where they can easily reach them. They also use pots of marginal plants sitting on pond shelves as fishing perches, often toppling them and muddying the water, if not actually catching some of the fish.

❦ Gardeners troubled by raccoons may elect to remove pots. A more drastic, but essentially harmless, measure is a low-voltage wire barrier, such as *Fido-Shock*, which deters raccoons and other small animals. It is, however, unsightly. Some gardeners recommend leaving a pair of well-used, smelly running shoes beside the pond — the odor is said to make raccoons cautious about approaching.

INTRODUCING FISH into THE GARDEN POND

❦ When you buy fish, make sure there's sufficient oxygen in the plastic bag containing your fish to let them survive the trip home. Pond suppliers often inject pure oxygen into the bag.

❦ Your pond should be ready for the fish — at the correct temperature, and treated with a dechlorinating product. Stock a new koi pond with just a few fish at first, so nitrifying bacteria become established in the biofilter.

❦ To equalize the temperature in the bag with that of the pond, leave the bag floating in the pond for 30 to 40 minutes, shading it with a wet towel to keep it from getting too hot.

❦ Don't let the fish out immediately; add a little pond water to the bag and seal it for 5 to 10 more minutes.

❦ When you release the fish, they will likely swim to the bottom. Don't be alarmed if you don't see them for a few days or more; they are familiarizing themselves with their new home.

❦ In a natural pond with some algae and assorted plants, goldfish don't generally require feeding. Once feeding habits are established, however, they should be adhered to regularly. All fish, but particularly koi, will become quite tame, eagerly approaching the hands that hold the food. Koi require special food and a regular feeding regimen. According to the season and the water temperature, there are even special protein/carbohydrate formulations.

❦ Invest in a good fish-care manual and check fish regularly for signs of fungal disease, bacterial infections, parasites or stress. The sight of fish coming to the surface to breathe indicates that there may be an insufficient oxygen level in the water. Use a pond-testing kit to monitor pond water for dangerous levels of ammonia and other toxins (see p. 87).

OTHER WATER FEATURES

WALL FOUNTAINS

A wall fountain introduces the delightful sound of trickling water to the smallest garden, solarium or apartment balcony. Water is pumped from a base receptacle or reservoir through a conduit (made of flexible tubing, rigid copper or PVC pipe) up into a drilled ornament through which the water then flows back into the receptacle. All you need are a strong wall or fence to support the unit or components, and a source of electrical power for the pump.

In the Middle Ages, decorative wall fountains called lavabos (from the Latin, *lavo*, which means to wash) were used in monasteries by monks as handwashing troughs. Classic marble lavabos can still be seen in the public squares of Rome and Florence.

Today, ready-made ornamental wall fountains are available in a variety of materials, sizes and styles and in a wide range of prices. There are one-piece Victorian reproductions in cast aluminum, featuring animal or gargoyle masks which spout into fluted shells or basins below. Tough, weatherproof polyethylene wall fountains have the look of old marble but are lightweight and easy to hang. An English firm specializing in classical garden ornaments offers a limestone dolphin which spouts into a scalloped stone bowl.

❧ To make your own wall fountain, fasten a pre-drilled spouted mask or ornament (or one you have drilled yourself using a masonry bit) to a sturdy wall, fence or screen within cord distance of a grounded electrical outlet.

❧ The base receptacle can be any watertight container such as a glazed ceramic bowl or planter, a clay pot without a drainage hole (or with the hole plugged with silicone caulking) or even a small formal pond. You can also create a below-ground reservoir by digging a hole and fitting it with a dark laundry tub or plastic garbage can. If desired, cover it with a decorative grate.

❧ Place a small recirculating pump in the base water receptacle, attaching it to a length of flexible PVC tubing. Bring the tubing out of the container and guide it up the wall (either behind it or, if in front, disguised by foliage, vines, metal tubing or wooden casing), then thread it through the hole in the upper ornament.

❧ When the pump is turned on, the water will flow through the spout back into the receptacle. A clamp can be used to adjust the flow to a pleasing trickle and to prevent it from splashing out of the receptacle.

PEBBLE POOLS *and* BUBBLE FOUNTAINS

These are effective low-maintenance water features, similar in principle to wall fountains, and are ideal for a patio or terrace. They're also a safe way to include water in a garden where there are small children.

❀ To make a pebble pool, start by digging out a small below-ground reservoir, then line it with flexible pond liner or fit it with a watertight container.

❀ Place a small submersible pump in the water, then plug it into a nearby grounded outlet. Attach a length of flexible tubing to the pump outlet and bring its end to the surface.

❀ Cover the excavation with a metal grate and thread the tubing through it. Pile smooth river rocks on top of the grate, pulling the tubing end to the upper surface of the rocks but making sure it isn't visible.

❀ When the pump is turned on, the water flows up through the rocks, bubbling up and splashing over them before cascading back into the reservoir.

❀ An old millstone makes an attractive bubble fountain, substituting for the river rocks mentioned above. Thread the tubing from the pump in the reservoir below, through the millstone's axle hole (which should be caulked at the surface to prevent water from seeping back down through it).

❀ Place the millstone atop the metal grate. When the pump is turned on, the water flows over the surface of the millstone, spilling over the sides and returning to the reservoir. If the millstone has a slight lip, the water will pool on the surface before spilling over the sides.

Horsetail rush (Equisetum spp.), an invasive plant in open water, takes on a very architectural appearance in a container, which also curbs its aggressive tendencies.

CONTAINER WATER GARDENS

It isn't necessary to excavate a pond in your garden in order to have water lilies or goldfish. Any watertight container can become a portable lily or fish pond. Provided you empty breakable containers in winter to prevent frost-cracking, this mini garden is remarkably easy to maintain.

❀ Potential containers include Oriental ginger or pickling jars, colorful ceramic or porcelain pots, basins, urns and even plastic planters. Wooden half whiskey barrels are inexpensive and have a rustic look; they can be lined with a flexible pond liner or fitted with a rigid fiberglass shell designed specifically for half-barrels. A container can be placed above ground or, for an interesting pond-like effect, sunk partially below it.

❀ Small hardy water lilies perfect for containers are yellow 'Pygmaea Helvola', white *Nymphaea tetragona* and bronze-orange 'Graziella'. 'Dauben' is a diminutive blue tropical lily that thrives in only a few inches of water. Dwarf cultivars of the sacred lotus, such as *Nelumbo* 'Momo Botan', are perfect for a half whiskey barrel, which is large enough for a few additional plants that can be raised to the appropriate depth on brick piers.

❀ Even without aquatic plants or fish, a handsome container filled with still water that reflects the sky and trees above adds an evocative, tranquil air to any garden setting.

POND MAINTENANCE THROUGH *the* SEASONS

SPRING

❦ It is not always necessary to clean out the pond. Very large ponds with thriving ecosystems seldom need cleaning, but small ponds with lots of plants usually need a partial water change and cleaning out in spring or fall.

❦ Gardeners who leave water lilies and fish to overwinter in deep water outdoors may choose to do maintenance in spring, as they divide aquatic plants and check on the condition of the fish. Others may wish to tidy the pond in autumn as they scoop out fallen leaves.

❦ If your pond exudes a foul odor and the water is dark when the ice melts in spring, there is a problem with rotting vegetation. Start by pumping approximately two-thirds of the volume out into adjacent flower beds, lawn or bog garden. If you used a de-icer through the winter, remove it. Remove fish and aquatic plants to a holding tank filled with the old pond water. Drain the rest of the water, removing debris with a sieve or wet-vac. Don't scrub pond walls too clean; they should retain some of their brown algae coating.

❦ Check that edging and waterfall rocks are still in alignment and that the liner at these points is cushioned with protective underlay.

❦ Flush out pumps, hoses and filters, and fill the pond with clean water, adding a dechlor agent if fish and plants are being held in temporary containment. The biofilter will take 4 to 5 weeks to establish nitrifying bacteria.

❦ Divide rootbound water lilies and aquatic plants, changing the soil and adding fertilizer tablets, if desired.

❦ Check water quality with a pond-testing kit before returning fish from the holding tank. If fish have been kept in an indoor aquarium during winter, put them in the pond only when the water temperature has reached 15°C (60°F), and acclimatize them slowly to the new water. Do not feed them until the water temperature reaches 18°C (64°F).

❦ When the water temperature reaches 15°C (60°F), hardy water lilies may be planted; wait until the water temperature reaches 20°C (70°F) before planting tropical water lilies. Start tropicals at 4 inches (10 cm) under the water surface, hardys 6 to 8 inches (15 to 20 cm), lowering them to their correct depth as water warms and new foliage reaches the water surface.

SUMMER

❦ Remove dead leaves and flowers from water lilies and fertilize every 4 weeks or when lily flowers or leaves become small, or new foliage has a yellowish look.

❦ Continue to monitor water quality with a pond-testing kit, especially during hot weather. If fish are seen gasping at the surface, increase oxygenation with an air pump.

❦ Replenish water lost through evaporation by spraying it in with a hose. Try not to replace more than

5 to 10 percent of water volume per week and use a dechlor product if fish are present and a greater volume is being replaced with tap water.

❀ Keep the pump free of sludge by cleaning out the mechanical pre-filter. When water flow through a biofilter decreases by 25 percent, remove the biofilter and quickly flush it with pond water. Do not use tap water on a biofilter once nitrifying bacteria are established.

❀ Thin out free-floating plants, such as duckweed, water hyacinth and water lettuce, to maintain a plant-free area that equals 30 to 40 percent of the pond's surface.

AUTUMN

❀ Use a pond net, if necessary, to prevent falling tree leaves from fouling the water. Submerged tree

leaves decompose underwater, releasing methane gas which can be fatal to fish. In a small pond, falling leaves can be removed daily with a hand skimmer.

❀ Cut back marginal aquatics (except for reeds, rushes and cattails, which help keep some of the surface water ice-free) after they've been

killed by frost. Move them to deeper water if you're overwintering them in the pond.

❀ Before the first frost, bring in tropical plants, such as papyrus, that will overwinter as house plants indoors. Cut back hardy and tropical water lily leaves and stems and bring indoors if pond is too shallow to prevent freezing; place lilies, still in their pots, in a plastic bag to keep them from drying out, and store at 5° to 10°C (40° to 50°F).

❀ Remove oxygenators and all free-floating plants; water hyacinths make good winter garden mulch.

❀ Do not feed fish after water temperature drops to 10°C (50°F). At this point, fish metabolism slows and they are unable to digest food. Unless you are overwintering fish in the pond, bring them indoors, acclimatizing them very gradually to

aquarium water. Remove filter and flexible tubing for use indoors if fish are brought in.

❀ If fish are to be overwintered in the pond, stop using the pump on the bottom, which can churn warm bottom water up to the surface. The pump can be lifted to near the surface where it will bubble, keeping

a small section ice-free. Alternatively, a floating de-icer can be used to keep a portion of the surface ice-free, so oxygen is admitted and toxic gases can escape. If desired, insulate the pond by covering it with plywood or foam insulation board topped with bags of leaves to try to prevent water from freezing solid.

WINTER

❀ If fish are overwintering in the pond, monitor it regularly to ensure that the de-icer is operating correctly. If the pond does freeze solid, do not bang on the ice to break it. This can cause concussion injury to fish. Use a cordless drill to make an opening, or pour boiling water over the surface to melt a hole.

❀ Check hardy and tropical water lilies being kept in cold storage indoors, watering if soil becomes dry. New growth on hardy lilies will be observed in late winter or early spring. Tropical lilies may not survive the winter. Consider it a bonus if they do.

TESTING POND WATER
❀

To ensure safe water quality for fish, especially in a koi pond, use a pond-testing kit which tests levels of ammonia, nitrite, nitrate and pH. When a tablet is added to a test tube of pond water, the resulting water color is compared to a chart which indicates whether levels are safe.

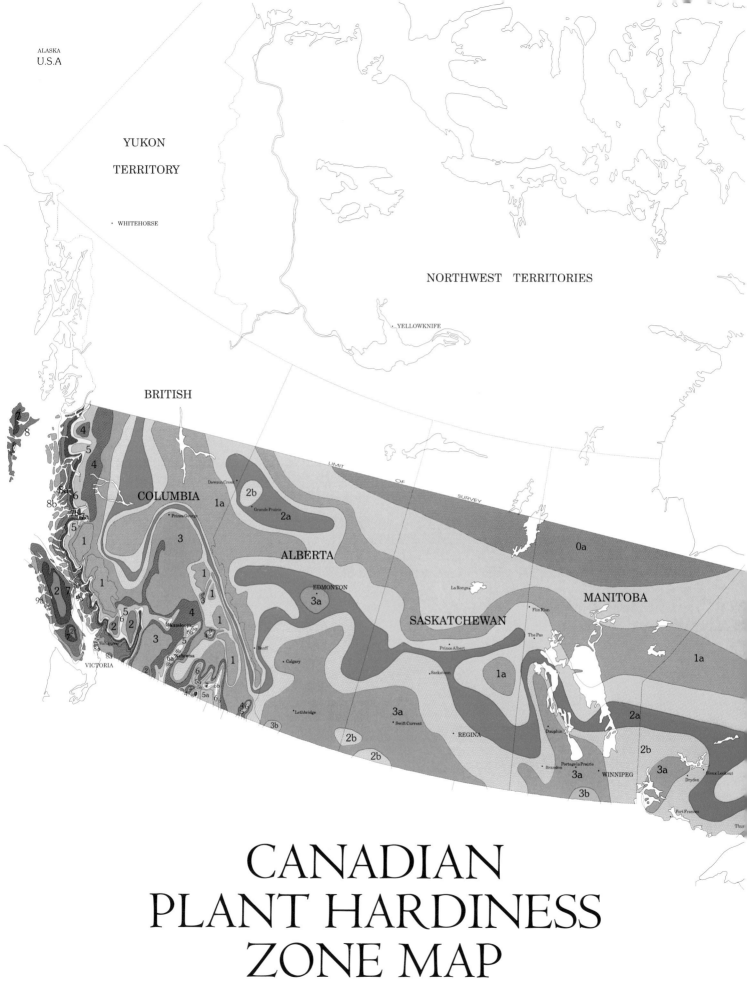

CANADIAN
PLANT HARDINESS
ZONE MAP

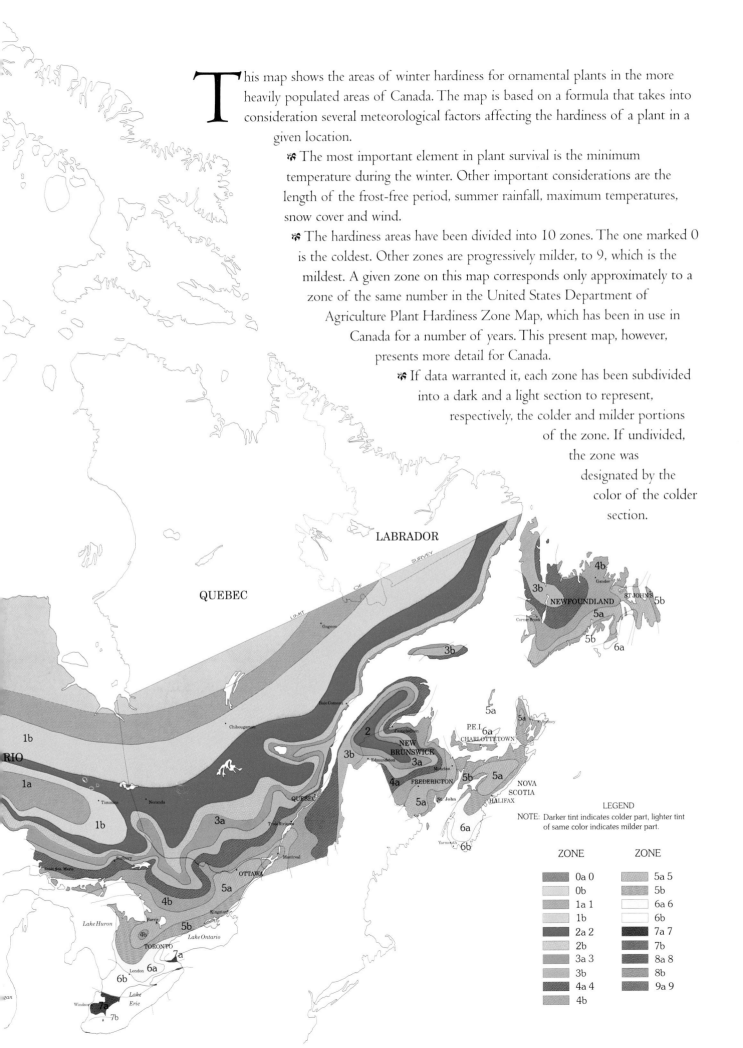

This map shows the areas of winter hardiness for ornamental plants in the more heavily populated areas of Canada. The map is based on a formula that takes into consideration several meteorological factors affecting the hardiness of a plant in a given location.

❧ The most important element in plant survival is the minimum temperature during the winter. Other important considerations are the length of the frost-free period, summer rainfall, maximum temperatures, snow cover and wind.

❧ The hardiness areas have been divided into 10 zones. The one marked 0 is the coldest. Other zones are progressively milder, to 9, which is the mildest. A given zone on this map corresponds only approximately to a zone of the same number in the United States Department of Agriculture Plant Hardiness Zone Map, which has been in use in Canada for a number of years. This present map, however, presents more detail for Canada.

❧ If data warranted it, each zone has been subdivided into a dark and a light section to represent, respectively, the colder and milder portions of the zone. If undivided, the zone was designated by the color of the colder section.

LABRADOR

QUEBEC

NEWFOUNDLAND

ST.JOHN'S

Gander

Corner Brook

NEW BRUNSWICK

P.E.I.

CHARLOTTETOWN

Sydney

Edmundston

FREDERICTON

Moncton

St. John

NOVA SCOTIA

HALIFAX

Yarmouth

LEGEND

NOTE: Darker tint indicates colder part, lighter tint of same color indicates milder part.

ZONE	ZONE
0a 0	5a 5
0b	5b
1a 1	6a 6
1b	6b
2a 2	7a 7
2b	7b
3a 3	8a 8
3b	8b
4a 4	9a 9
4b	

THE CONTRIBUTORS

JANET DAVIS has been in love with gardening since she sniffed her first wallflower, at the age of two, in Victoria, B.C. A freelance writer and photographer now living in Toronto, her work has been featured in *Canadian Gardening* and in other magazines including *Canadian Living, Chatelaine Gardens, Toronto Life Gardens, Fine Gardening, Toronto Gardens* and *Leisureways.* Her Saturday column, Into The Garden, runs spring through fall in *The Toronto Sun.* She was Landscape Ontario's 1995 Garden Communicator of the Year.

LIZ PRIMEAU is editor-in-chief of *Canadian Gardening* and host of Canadian Gardening Television on Life network. In her six years with the magazine, she has visited gardens in all parts of Canada and has heard firsthand from committed Canadian gardeners about what works — or doesn't work! — in this widely varied climate of ours. An avid and experienced gardener herself, she has also been a featured speaker at gardening conferences, trade shows and garden clubs. Liz Primeau writes regularly on gardening for *The Globe and Mail's* Design section, and has also worked as a writer and editor with *Weekend Magazine, Toronto Life, Chatelaine, City Woman, Vista* and *Ontario Living* during her 24-year journalistic career.

Photographers

HARRISON BAKER: page 57.

TREVOR COLE: page 45 (top).

JANET DAVIS: pages 1, 3, 4, 14, 21, 27, 28, 30, 43, 44, 50, 53, 56, 60, 62, 63, 64, 66, 69, 75, 76, 77 (middle and right), 78 (left and bottom right), 79, 80, 81, 82, 85.

JOHN DE VISSER: page 11.

CHRISTOPHER DEW: front cover; pages 8, 12, 15, 24, 35, 49, 52, 70-71, 73, 86-87.

JIM EAGER: page 84.

ADAM GIBBS: pages 16, 34, 37, 45 (bottom).

DAVID INGLIS: page 67.

FRANK KERSHAW: pages 7, 17.

BERT KLASSEN: photo of Liz Primeau; page 96 (background).

PAT LACROIX: page 46.

MARILYNN McARA: pages 19, 32, 51, 58, 77 (left), 78 (top right).

JOHN SCANLAN: page 18.

LYNN THOMPSON: page 23.

PADDY WALES: pages 9, 10.

All illustrations are by CAROL PATON, a Toronto artist who specializes in botanical watercolors.

The map of Canada's Plant Hardiness Zones (pages 88-89) was produced by the Centre for Land and Biological Resources Research, Agriculture Canada, from information supplied by the Ottawa Research Station and the Meteorological Branch, Environment Canada 1993. We would like to thank Bryan Monette and Ron St. John of the Research Branch for their kind help in supplying this material.

Acknowledgments

We are indebted to the many gardeners whose properties appear throughout this book. Our thanks to John Ceraldi, Sheila Clark, Susan Collacott, Ann Collombin (design by Ernie Haynes and Doug McClure), Paul Cotterill (design by Mark Hartley), Donna Dawson, Brian Folmer, Pam and Jim Gordon (design by Joe Ottmann and Charles Mattson), Kent Gullickson, Elizabeth and George Knowles, Ernie Koch, Dr. Lambert, Joan Langley, Terry Le Blanc, Mrs. Mary Mello, Hélène Morneau, Doug Murray, Orto Botanico, Liliana Perodeau, Picov's Water Gardens, Wayne Renaud, Dr. Glen Renecker (design by Neil Turnbull), Linda Schafhauser, Ken Shimada, Muriel and Merrill Stafford, and Amy and Clare Stewart.

✤ In some cases, it was not possible to identify gardens or their owners. We acknowledge them here and are grateful for the use of this material.

SPECIAL THANKS

✤ Successful water gardening is equal parts aesthetics, biology, engineering and horticulture. For sharing their expertise in one or more of these areas, I am grateful to Barry Greig of the University of Alberta's Devonian Botanic Garden; Terry Fahey; Sue See of Moore's Water Gardens, Port Stanley, Ontario; Henry Reimer of Reimer's Waterscapes, Tillsonburg, Ontario; Tom Thomson of Humber Nurseries, Brampton, Ontario; and Toronto landscape architect Neil Turnbull. My warm thanks to Ray Shivrattan of Picov's Water Gardens in Ajax, Ontario, for providing access to Picov's excellent demonstration gardens and for taking the time to review the manuscript. My thanks also to Carol Paton, for her lovely illustrations showing us what goes on under the water; and to Trevor Cole, for casting a sharp horticultural eye over the manuscript. To Liz Primeau, my heartfelt appreciation for her peerless editorial instincts and her enthusiasm for the project. And to project editor Wanda Nowakowska of Madison Press, my most sincere thanks for being an unflappable model of efficiency, organization and unfailing good humor.

— *Janet Davis*

✤ This is really Janet Davis's book, full of her ideas and personal knowledge of garden ponds as well as her exhaustive research. The text is also blessed with her inherent writing skill, and I want to thank her here for all of the above. Of course, we couldn't have published this without the guidance and basic book smarts of Wanda Nowakowska, Madison Press assistant editorial director and project editor of the series, or the art direction of Gordon Sibley. Special thanks, too, to Brenda and Trevor Cole, who provided the expert eyes that checked the text, and to all the photographers who so willingly submitted their work for this project. I am also grateful to Tom Hopkins, editorial director of *Canadian Gardening*, and Phil Whalen, its publisher, without whom none of this would be possible.

— *Liz Primeau*

Selected Bibliography

✤ Allison, James. *Water in the Garden*. Boston: Little, Brown, 1991.

✤ Archer-Wills, Anthony. *The Water Gardener*. New York: Barron's Educational Series, 1993.

✤ Archibald, David, and Marry Patton, ed. *Harrowsmith Gardener's Guide: Water Gardens*. Camden East, Ontario: Camden House, 1990.

✤ Glattstein, Judy. *Waterscaping*. Pownal, Vermont: Storey Communications, 1994.

✤ Greenoak, Francesca. *Water Features for Small Gardens*. Vancouver: Cavendish Books, 1996.

✤ Grinstain, Dawn Tucker. *Pools, Ponds and Waterways*. Toronto: Penguin Books Canada, 1992.

✤ Heritage, Bill. *Ponds and Water Gardens*. Poole, U.K.: Blandford Press, 1981.

✤ Nash, Helen. *The Complete Pond Builder*. New York: Sterling Publishing, 1996.

✤ Nash, Helen. *The Pond Doctor*. New York: Sterling Publishing, 1994.

✤ Perry, Frances. *The Water Garden*. London: Ward Lock Limited, 1981.

✤ Rae-Smith, William. *The Complete Book of Water Gardening*. London: Bracken Books, 1989.

✤ Stadelman, Peter. *Water Gardens*. New York: Barron's Educational Series, 1991.

✤ Swindells, Philip. *At the Water's Edge*. London: Ward Lock Limited, 1988.

✤ van Sweden, James. *Gardening with Water*. New York: Random House, 1995.

✤ Wilson, Andrew. *The Creative Water Gardener*. London: Ward Lock Limited, 1995.

INDEX

E

Echinodorus cordifolius, 80, *80*
Ecology, 20
Ecosystem, 20, 86
Edging, 37, 38, 41
    stones, 38, 39, *41*
    plants, 41
Eel grass, 76
Eichornia crassipes, 30
    E. crassipes major, 76, *76*
Elderberry, 47
Electrical outlets, 17, 85
Electricity, 17, 44
Eleocharis montevidensis, 79
Elephant's ear, 80
Elodea, 25, 30, 68
    E. canadensis, 31, 76
Emergent aquatic plants,
    68, 77
EPDM pond liner, 39, 63
Equisetum spp., 85
Euonymus, 45
Evening primrose, 79
Evergreen hedges, 45
Evergreens, 41

F

Fairy moss, 76
False cypress, 56
Fancy goldfish, 82
Fantails, 82
Fens, 62
Ferns, 17, 47, 63
Fertilizer tablets, 86

Fiberglass pond shell, 63, 85
Filters, 26, 27, 44, 87
Filtration system, 25
Fish, 9, 19, *20,* 22, *24,* 25,
    26, 28, 30, 31, 34, 40,
    44, 68, 69, 76, 82,
    83, 86
    barriers, *27*
    controlling
        population, 26
    feeding, 26, 82
    goldfish, 9, 10
    introducing to pond, 83
    metabolism, 87
    overwintering, 35, 82
    stocking a new pond, 26
    toxic plants, 17
Flagstones, *41*
Floating heart, 68, 79, *79*
Floating plants, 22, *30*
Flowering rush, 78
Flowering shrubs, 45
Formal reflecting pool, 19
Fountains, *3,* 17, 25, 85
    kits, 9
Fragrant sumac, 56
Free-floating aquatic plants,
    68, 76
Fringetails, 82
Frog's bit, 76

G

Geese, 83
Geotextile pond liner,
    39, 63
Ginkgo, 45
Globeflower, 17
Glyceria aquatica 'Variegata', 78
Golden club, 81
Golden orfees, 82
Goldfish, 25, 35, 76, 82, 85
    common, 82
Graceful cattail, 78
Grasses, 78
Gravel beach, 38
Great blue lobelia, 62, 77
Green taro, 80
Ground covers, 56

H

Hardy marginal aquatic
    plants, 77
Hardy water lilies, 86, 87
Hemlock, 45, 56
Hibiscus moscheutos, 79
    H. moscheutos 'Southern
        Belle', 79
    H. palustris, 79
Highbush blueberry, 60
Hornwort, 25, 30, 31,
    68, 76
Horsetail, 62
Horsetail rush, 85
Hostas, 17, *43,* 47, 56
Houttuynia cordata, 77
Hydrocharis morsus-ranae, 76
Hydrocleyes nymphoides, 77
Hymenocallis liriosme, 81

I

Imperial taro, 80
Irises, 8, 9
    blue water, 78
    I. pseudacorus, 17, 69, 79
    I. pseudacorus
        'Variegata', 79
    I. versicolor, 69, 78
    Japanese, 47, *60, 63*
    lavendar-blue, 69
    Siberian, 47, *56*
    water, 69
    yellow flag, 47
    yellow water, 79
Irish moss, 56
Ironwood, 47
Irrigation, 63
Italian Renaissance
    gardens, 11

J

Japanese blood grass, 47
Japanese cherry, 45
Japanese iris, 17, *60, 63*
Japanese landscape
    design, 11
Japanese maple, 45, *47,*
    53, 56
Japanese primrose, 17
Japanese sedge, 56
Juncus effusus 'Spiralis', 78
Jussiaea diffusa, 79

K

Kalmia polifolia, 60
Katsura, 45
Kent, William, 11
Knotweed, 56
Koi, 25, 26, *27,* 35, 82,
    83, 87

L

Labrador tea, 60
Lady's-mantle, 41, *56*
Landscapes, 11
Landscaping, 45
    Oriental, 45
Laurel, 45
Ledum groenlandicum, 60
Lemna minor, 76
Lighting, 44
Ligularia, 17
Liner, 36, 59, 63, 85
    calculating amount, 38
    types, 39
Lionheads, 82
Lizard's tail, 79
Lobelia cardinalis, 77, *77*
    L. siphilitica, 77
Lotuses, 68, 75
    cultivars, 75
    dwarf cultivars, 85
    Yellow American , 75
Lythrum salicaria, 47
    L. virgatum, 47

EDITORIAL DIRECTOR   Hugh Brewster

PROJECT EDITOR   Wanda Nowakowska

EDITORIAL ASSISTANCE   Rebecca Hanes-Fox

PRODUCTION DIRECTOR   Susan Barrable

PRODUCTION COORDINATOR   Sandra L. Hall

BOOK DESIGN AND LAYOUT   Gordon Sibley Design Inc.

PRINTING AND BINDING   Tien Wah Press

CANADIAN GARDENING'S
WATER *in the* GARDEN
was produced by
Madison Press Books